FROM
Farm Boy to Senator

BEING THE HISTORY
OF THE
Boyhood and Manhood of Daniel Webster

BY

HORATIO ALGER, JR.
AUTHOR OF
"FROM CANAL BOY TO PRESIDENT," "DEAN DUNHAM,"
"THE $500 CHECK," ETC.

**Fredonia Books
Amsterdam, The Netherlands**

From Farm Boy to Senator:
The History of the Boyhood and Manhood of Daniel Webster

by
Horatio Alger, Jr.

ISBN: 1-4101-0618-7

Copyright © 2004 by Fredonia Books

Reprinted from the 1882 edition

Fredonia Books
Amsterdam, The Netherlands
http://www.fredoniabooks.com

All rights reserved, including the right to reproduce this book, or portions thereof, in any form.

In order to make original editions of historical works available to scholars at an economical price, this facsimile of the original edition of 1882 is reproduced from the best available copy and has been digitally enhanced to improve legibility, but the text remains unaltered to retain historical authenticity.

TO

MY FRIEND AND COLLEGE CLASSMATE,

JUDGE ADDISON BROWN,

OF NEW YORK,

THIS VOLUME IS CORDIALLY INSCRIBED.

PREFACE.

But thirty years have elapsed since the death of Daniel Webster, and there is already danger that, so far as young people are concerned, he will become an historic reminiscence. Schoolboys, who declaim the eloquent extracts from his speeches which are included in all the school speakers, are indeed able to form some idea of his great oratorical powers and the themes which called them forth; but I have found that young classical students, as a rule, know more of Cicero's life than of his. It seems to me eminently fitting that the leading incidents in the life of our great countryman, his struggles for an education, the steps by which he rose to professional and political distinction, should be made familiar to American boys. I have therefore essayed a "story biography," which I have tried to write in such a manner as to make it attractive to young people, who are apt to turn away from ordinary biographies, in the fear that they may prove dull.

I have not found my task an easy one. Webster's life is so crowded with great services and events, it is so interwoven with the history of the nation, that to give a fair idea of him in a volume of ordinary size is almost impossible. I have found it necessary to leave out some things, and to refer briefly to others, lest my book should expand to undue proportions. Let me acknowledge then, with the utmost frankness, that my work is incomplete, and necessarily so. This causes me less regret, because those whom I may be fortunate enough to interest in my subject will readily find all that they wish to know in the noble Life of Webster, by George Ticknor Curtis, the captivating Reminiscences, by Peter Harvey, the Private Correspondence, edited by Fletcher Webster, and the collection of Mr. Webster's speeches, edited by Mr. Everett. They will also find interesting views of Mr. Webster's senatorial career in the Reminiscences of Congress, by Charles W. March.

If this unpretending volume shall contribute in any way to extend the study of Mr. Webster's life and works, I shall feel that my labor has been well bestowed.

HORATIO ALGER, JR.

FROM FARM BOY TO SENATOR.

A BOYS' LIFE OF
DANIEL WEBSTER.

CHAPTER I.

THE COTTON HANDKERCHIEF.

"WHERE are you going, Daniel?"

"To Mr. Hoyt's store."

"I'll go in with you. Where is 'Zekiel this morning?"

"I left him at work on the farm."

"I suppose you will both be farmers when you grow up?"

"I don't know," answered Daniel, thoughtfully. "I don't think I shall like it, but there isn't anything else to do in Salisbury."

"You might keep a store, and teach school like Master Hoyt."

"Perhaps so. I should like it better than farming."

Daniel was but eight years old, a boy of striking appearance, with black hair and eyes, and a swarthy complexion. He was of slender frame, and his large dark eyes, deep set beneath an overhanging brow, gave a singular appearance to the thin face of the delicate looking boy.

He was a farmer's son, and lived in a plain, old-fashioned house, shaded by fine elms, and separated from the broad, quiet street by a fence. It was situated in a valley, at the bend of the Merrimac, on both sides of which rose high hills, which the boy climbed many a time for the more extended view they commanded. From a high sheep-pasture on his father's farm, through a wide opening in the hills, he could see on a clear day Ascutney Mountain in Vermont, and in a different direction the snowy top of Mount Washington, far away to the northeast.

He entered the humble store with his companion.

Behind the counter stood Master Hoyt, a tall man, of stern aspect, which could strike terror into the hearts of delinquent scholars when in the winter they came to receive instruction from him.

"Good morning, Daniel," said Master Hoyt, who was waiting upon a customer.

"Good morning, sir," answered Daniel, respectfully.

"I hope you won't forget what you learned at school last winter."

"No, sir, I will try not to."

"You mustn't forget your reading and writing."

"No, sir; I read whatever I can find, but I don't like writing much."

"You'll never make much of a hand at writing, Daniel. Ezekiel writes far better than you. But you won't need writing much when you're following the plough."

"I hope I shan't have to do that, Master Hoyt."

"Ay, you're hardly strong enough, you may find something else to do in time. You may keep school like me—who knows?—but you'll have to get some one else to set the copies," and Master Hoyt laughed, as if he thought it a good joke.

Daniel listened gravely to the master's prediction, but it seemed to him he should hardly care to be a teacher like Mr. Hoyt, for the latter, though he was a good reader, wrote an excellent hand, and had a slight knowledge of grammar, could carry his pupils no further. No pupil was likely to wonder that "one small head could carry all he knew." Yet the boys respected him, and in his limited way he did them good.

Master Hoyt had by this time finished waiting upon his customer, and was at leisure to pay attention to his two young callers. He regarded them rather as pupils than as customers, for it is quite the custom in sparsely settled neighborhoods to "drop in" at the store for a chat.

Meanwhile Daniel's roving eyes had been attracted by a cotton pocket-handkerchief, which appeared to have something printed upon it.

Master Hoyt noticed the direction of the boy's gaze.

"I see you are looking at the handkerchief," he said. "Would you like to see what is printed on it?"

"Yes, sir."

The handkerchief was taken down and placed in the boy's hands. It was quite customary in those days, when books and papers were comparatively rare and difficult to obtain, to combine literature with plain homely utility, by printing reading matter of some kind on cheap cotton handkerchiefs. Nowadays boys would probably object to such a custom, but the boy, Daniel who was fond of reading, was attracted.

"Is it a story?" he asked.

"No, Daniel; it is the Constitution of the United States—the government we live under."

Daniel's interest was excited. Of the government he knew something, but not much, and up to that moment he had not known that there was a constitution, and indeed he couldn't tell what a constitution was, but he thought he would like to know.

"What is the price?" he asked.

"Twenty-five cents."

Daniel felt in his pocket, and drew out a quarter of a dollar. It represented all his worldly wealth. It had not come to him all at once, but was the accumulation of pennies saved. He may have had other plans for spending it, but now when there was a chance of securing something to read he could not resist the temptation, so he passed over his precious coin, and the handkerchief became his.

"It's a good purchase," said Master Hoyt, approvingly. "Take it home, Daniel, and read it, and you'll know something of the government we're living under. I suppose you've heard your father talk of the days when he was a soldier, and fought against the British?"

"Yes, sir."

"When soldiers were called for, Captain Webster was one of the first to answer the call. But of course you are too young to remember that time."

"Yes, sir: but I have heard father talk about it."

"Ay, ay; your father was selected to stand guard before General Washington's headquarters on the night after Arnold's treason. The general knew he could depend upon him."

"Yes, sir; I am sure of that," said the boy proudly, for he had a high reverence and respect for his soldier father, who on his side was devoted to the best interests of his sons, and was ready when the time came to make sacrifices for them such as would have made most fathers hesitate.

"Ah, those were dark days, Daniel. You are lucky to live in peaceful times, under a free government, but you must never forget how your father and other brave men fought to secure the blessings we now enjoy. Now General Washington is President, and we are no longer a subject colony, but we have a free and independent government."

It is doubtful how far Daniel and his young companion understood the remarks of Master Hoyt, but doubtless a time came further on when the words recurred to him, and in the light of his father's conversations, which from time to time he held with his neighbors, gave him a more adequate idea of the character of that government in which in after years he was to take so prominent a part.

"Are you going, Daniel?" asked William

Hoyt, as the boys turned to leave his humble store.

"Yes, sir; father may want me at home."

"Don't forget your learning, my lad. You must be ready to take up your studies next winter. Soon you will know as much as I do."

It was meant for an encouraging remark, but the prospect it held out was not one to dazzle the imagination even of a boy of eight, for as I have already said the good man's acquirements were of the most limited character.

Daniel went home with his precious handkerchief snugly stowed away in his pocket. He was saving it till evening when he promised himself the pleasure of reading it.

After supper by the light of the open log fire he brought out his new possession.

"What have you there, my son?" asked his father.

"It is a handkerchief, father, with the Constitution of the United States printed on it."

"Where did you get it?"

"At Master Hoyt's store."

"Dan spent all his money for it," said Ezekiel.

"Well, well, he might have done worse. It will do him no harm to read the Constitution of his country," said the father, gravely.

Thus assured of his father's approval, the boy

devoted himself to the reading of that famous document, of which in after years he was to become the staunch supporter and defender. For this boy was in his manhood to rank among the great men of the earth, and to leave a name and a fame to which his countrymen for centuries to come will point with just and patriotic pride.

This boy with slender form, swarthy face, and dark eyes, was Daniel Webster.

CHAPTER II.

DANIEL AND HIS FATHER.

Daniel's family had not lived many years at Elms Farm. Captain Webster first occupied a log house which he had himself built, and in this humble dwelling Ezekiel and one of his sisters were born. He was poor in worldly goods, but rich in children, having had ten born to him, five by the second marriage. Daniel was the youngest but one, and Sarah the youngest of all.

When the war of the American Revolution broke out Daniel's father was one of the first to take up arms. He himself drew up, and induced eighty-four of his townsmen to sign, the following patriotic pledge:

"We do solemnly engage and promise that we will, to the utmost of our power, at the risk of our lives and fortunes, with arms, oppose the hostile proceedings of the British fleets and armies against the United American Colonies."

Daniel was proud of his descent from such a man, and in the last year of his life declared that "this is sufficient emblazonry for my arms; enough of heraldry for me."

Ebenezer Webster, Daniel's father, is described as "a man of great firmness, whose bearing and manner were decisive; tall and erect, with a full chest, black hair and eyes, and rather large and prominent features." He had never attended school, but his natural powers, supplemented by his own persistent efforts for education, qualified him for a high and influential place in the community in which he lived. But in one thing he was lacking, the ability to make money, and was obliged to practise the utmost frugality in his household. Though he filled various important positions, his compensation was of the smallest. He charged the town for important services but three or four shillings a day—a sum which even the most modest of office-holders nowadays would regard as quite beneath their acceptance.

How he succeeded in wresting a subsistence for his large family from his sterile acres must remain a mystery. He was willing to live poorly, but there was one subject which cost him anxious thought. How was he to provide his family, and especially the two youngest boys, with the educational advantages which had been denied to him? There were no good schools near home, and without money he could not send his boys out of town to school.

Help came in an unexpected way.

One day the stalwart farmer entered his house with a look of satisfaction on his dark and rugged features.

"Wife," he said, "I have been appointed Judge of the Court of Common Pleas for the county."

"Indeed!" said his wife, naturally pleased at the honor which had been conferred upon her husband.

"It will bring me three to four hundred dollars a year," said Mr. Webster, "and now I can hope to educate my boys."

This was his first thought, and hers. It was not proposed to improve their style of living, to buy new furniture or new clothes, but to spend it in such a way as would best promote the interests of those whom God had committed to their keeping.

Three or four hundred dollars! It was a very small sum, so most of my boy readers will think; and so it was, but in a farmer's household on the bleak acres of New Hampshire it would go a considerable way. Every dollar in Ebenezer Webster's hands brought its money's worth, and as we shall see hereafter it brought rich interest to the investor.

But Daniel was still too young for any immediate steps to be taken in the desired direction. He was sent to the small town schools, where he learned what the master was able to teach him. Sometimes he had two and a half and three miles to walk to school, but the farmer's boy, though delicate, was not thought too delicate for such a walk. Indeed the boy's delicacy was in his favor, for he was thought not robust enough to work on the farm steadily, and was sent to school, as an elder half-brother, Joseph, laughingly said, "to make him equal with the rest of the boys." It was hard for those who saw him in later years, in his majestic proportions, to believe that he had been a delicate boy. The tender sapling had become a stately oak, with not a trace of feebleness or lack of strength.

One day when Daniel was at work in the hayfield, about the middle of the forenoon, Judge Webster, for this was his designation now, saw a carriage approaching.

"Some one to see you, father," suggested Daniel.

"Yes," said his father, preparing to leave his work; "it is the Congressman from our district."

"What is his name?"

"Hon. Abiel Foster, my son. He lives in Canterbury."

But the Congressman descended from his carriage and entered the field where Daniel and his father were at work. "Don't let me interrupt you, Judge Webster," said the visitor. "I merely wished to exchange a few words on public affairs."

Daniel was old enough to have some notion of the office of a Congressman and his duties, and he regarded the honorable gentleman with attention, and perhaps with reverent respect, though he is said not to have been endowed with more than average ability, notwithstanding he had been educated at college, and had once been a minister.

When the conversation was over the Congressman got into his carriage and rode away. Judge Webster looked thoughtfully after him.

Then he said to Daniel, "My son, that is a worthy man; he is a Member of Congress; he goes to Philadelphia, and gets six dollars a day, while I toil here. It is because he had an education which I never had. If I had had his early education I should have been in Philadelphia in his place. I came near it as it was. But I missed it, and now I must work here."

"My dear father," answered Daniel, not without emotion, "you shall not work. Brother and I will work for you, and will wear our hands out, and you shall rest."

The boy was much moved, and his breast heaved, for he knew well how hard his father had toiled for him and for all the family.

"My child," said Judge Webster, "it is of no importance to me. I now live but for my children. I could not give your elder brothers the advantages of knowledge, but I can do something for you. Exert yourself, improve your opportunities, learn, learn, and when I am gone you will not need to go through the hardships which I have undergone, and which have made me an old man before my time."

These words made a profound impression upon the boy. A man's character and life add weight to the words which he utters, and wise and judicious advice coming from a trifler or a shallow person falls often unheeded, and with reason. But Daniel knew how much his father had accomplished without education—he knew how high his rank was among his neighbors, and no man ever probably received from him a tithe of that reverence which he felt for his plain, unlettered parent.

By this time he knew that his father had been largely instrumental in inducing New Hampshire to ratify that Constitution of which he obtained his first knowledge from the cheap cotton handkerchief which he had purchased at Master Hoyt's store. The acceptance was by no means a foregone conclusion. Many of the delegates to the convention had been instructed to vote against acceptance, and among them Ebenezer Webster himself. But he obtained permission later to vote according to his own judgment, and the speech which he made in favor of this important action has been preserved. Just before the vote was taken, he rose and said:

"Mr. President, I have listened to the arguments for and against the Constitution. I am convinced such a government as that Constitution will establish, if adopted—a government acting directly on the people of the States—is necessary for the common defence and the public welfare. It is the only government which will enable us to pay off the national debt—the debt which we owe for the Revolution, and which we are bound in honor fully and fairly to discharge. Besides, I have followed the lead of Washington through seven years of war, and I have never been misled. His name is subscribed to this Constitution. He will not mislead us now. I shall vote for its adoption."

No wonder that Daniel inherited from his father a reverent attachment for that Constitution which Judge Webster by word and deed had helped to secure and establish. His father was a grave and earnest man, but he was not stern nor ascetic. His strength was softened by good humor, and his massive features were often lighted up by a contagious laugh which endeared him to his family, who loved no less than they respected him.

CHAPTER III.

A MEMORABLE BATTLE.

DANIEL, as well as his father, had a love of fun, and a sportive humor, which he always preserved. It is said that "all work and no play makes Jack a dull boy." It is certainly a mistake when a boy is shut out from the innocent sports which boys delight in. John Stuart Mill, who was set to learning while little more than an infant, and who actually began to study Greek at four years of age—lamented in after years that he had never known what boyhood was.

It was not so with Daniel. Though his father's poverty made it necessary for all to work, Daniel, partly because of his early delicacy, had plenty of time allowed him for amusement. The favorite companion of his leisure hours was not a boy, but a veteran soldier and near neighbor, named Robert Wise. He had built a little cottage in the corner of the Webster farm, and there with his wife he lived till extreme old age. He was born in Yorkshire, had fought on both sides in the Revolutionary struggle, had travelled in various parts of Europe, and had a thousand stories to tell, to all of which the boy listened with avidity. Though he had twice deserted from the English king, his heart still thrilled with pride when Daniel read to him from the newspaper accounts of battles in which the English arms were victorious. He had never learned to read, and Daniel became his favorite because he was always ready to read to him as they sat together at nightfall at the cottage door.

"Why don't you learn to read yourself, Robert?" asked Daniel one day.

"It's too late, Dan. I'm gettin' an old man now, and I couldn't do it."

"What will you do when I am grown up, and gone away?"

"I don't know, Dan. It will be dull times for me."

When that time came the old man picked up a fatherless boy, and gave him a home and a chance to secure an education, in order that he might have some one to read the newspaper to him.

Whenever Daniel had a day or a few hours to himself he ran across the fields to his humble neighbor's house.

"Come, Robert," he would say, "I've got nothing to do. Let us go fishing."

So the two would go down to the banks of the Merrimac, and embark in a boat which belonged to the old man, and paddle up and down the river, sometimes for an entire day. Daniel never lost his love of fishing, but in after years, when the cares of statesmanship were upon him, dressed in suitable style he would take his fishing pole and lie in wait for his finny victims, while perhaps he was mentally composing some one of his famous speeches, destined to thrill the hearts of thousands, or direct the policy of the government. These happy days spent in the open air corrected his native delicacy, and gradually imparted physical strength and vigor, and in time knit the vigorous frame which seemed a fitting temple for his massive intellect.

Even the most trivial circumstances in the boyhood of such a man as Daniel Webster are noteworthy, and I am sure my boy-readers will read with interest and sympathy the account of a signal victory which the boy gained, though it was only over a feathered bully.

Belonging to a neighbor was a cock of redoubtable prowess, a champion whose fame was in all the farmyards for miles around. One day Daniel, coming home from school, beheld with mortification the finish of a contest in which a favorite fowl of his own came off decidedly second best.

The victorious rooster strutted about in conscious and complacent triumph.

"It's too bad, Zeke!" said Daniel in genuine vexation, as he saw the crestfallen look of his own vanquished fowl. "I should like to see that impudent bully get well whipped."

"There isn't a rooster about here that can whip him, Dan."

"I know that, but he will meet his match some time."

"At any rate I'll drive him away. He'll have to run from me."

Dan picked up a stone, and pelted the victor out of the yard, but the feathered bully, even in his flight, raised a crow of victory which vexed the boy.

"I'd give all the money I've got, Zeke, for a rooster that would whip him," said Dan.

There came a time when Daniel had his wish.

He was visiting a relation at some distance when mention was made casually of a famous fighting cock who had never been beaten.

"Where is he to be found?" asked the boy eagerly.

"Why do you ask?"

"I would like to see him," said Dan.

"Oh, well, he belongs to Mr. ——."

"Where does he live?"

The desired information was given.

Shortly after Daniel was missed. He found his way to the farm where the pugnacious fowl resided. In the yard he saw the owner, a farmer.

"Good morning, sir," said Dan.

"Good morning, boy. What can I do for you?" was the reply.

"I hear you have a cock who is a famous fighter."

"Yes, he's never been beaten yet!" said the farmer complacently.

"Can I see him?"

"There he is," said the owner, pointing out the feathered champion.

Daniel surveyed the rooster with great interest.

"Will you sell him?" he asked.

"I don't know. Why do you want to buy him?"

Daniel explained his object frankly.

"How much are you willing to give?" asked the farmer, for he was a Yankee, and ready for a trade.

Daniel drew from his pocket half a dollar. It represented his entire cash capital.

"Here is half a dollar," he said. "I'll give you that."

"Haven't you got any more money?" asked the farmer, who had a keen scent for a bargain.

"No, sir; it is all I have. I'd give you more if I had it."

Half a dollar in those days was a considerable sum of money, particularly in the eyes of a farmer, who handled very little money, his income being for the most part in the shape of corn, hay and vegetables. Having satisfied himself that it was all he could get, he gave a favorable answer to the boy's application.

Daniel's eyes sparkled with delight, and he promptly handed over his fifty cent piece.

"When do you want to take it?" asked the farmer.

"Now," answered Dan.

"Very well."

The fowl was caught, and Daniel carried it back to the house of his relative in triumph.

"I'm going home," he said abruptly.

"Going home? Why, you have only just come."

"I'll come again soon, but I want to take this cock home, and see if he can't whip Mr. ——'s. I want to teach the little bully a lesson."

So in spite of all that could be said Daniel started on his way home.

When he had gone a short distance he passed

a yard stocked with poultry, where a large cock was strutting about defiantly, as if throwing down the gage of battle to any new comers.

A boy was standing near the fence.

"Will your cock fight?" asked Dan.

"He can whip yours," was the reply.

"Are you willing to try it?"

"Yes, come along."

The trial was made, and Dan's new purchase maintained his reputation, by giving a sound drubbing to his feathered rival.

Dan surveyed the result with satisfaction.

"I guess he'll do," he said to himself.

He kept on his way till he got within sight of home.

"What brings you home so soon, Dan?" asked Zeke.

"See here, Zeke!" said Dan eagerly. "Here is a cock that will whip Mr ——'s all to pieces."

"Don't be too sure of it!"

"I've tried him once, and he's game."

The boys did not have long to wait for the trial.

Over came the haughty intruder, strutting about with his usual boastful air.

Dan let loose his new fowl, and a battle royal commenced. Soon the tyrant of the barn-yard found that he had met a foe worthy of his spur. For a time the contest was an open one, but in ten minutes the feathered bully was ignominiously defeated, and led about by the comb in a manner as humiliating as had ever happened when he was himself the victor.

Daniel witnessed the defeat of the whilom tyrant with unbounded delight, and felt abundantly repaid for his investment of all his spare cash, as well as the cutting short of his visit. Probably in the famous passage at arms which he had many years after with Mr. Hayne, of South Carolina, his victory afforded him less satisfaction than this boyish triumph.

CHAPTER IV.

AN IMPORTANT STEP.

"WHAT are you thinking about, Dan?" asked his mother one evening as the boy sat thoughtfully gazing at the logs blazing in the fireplace.

"I was wishing for something to read," answered the boy.

Indeed that was his chief trouble in those early days. Libraries were scarce, and private collections equally scarce, especially in small country places. So the boy's appetite for books was not likely to be satisfied.

Daniel's words attracted the attention of his father.

"I have been speaking to some of our neighbors to-day," he said, "about establishing a small circulating library which we could all use. I think we shall do something about it soon."

"I hope you will, father," said Dan eagerly.

"If we all contribute a little, we can make a beginning. Besides we can put in some books we have already."

A week or two later Judge Webster announced that the library had been established, and it may be easily supposed that Daniel was one of the first to patronize it. It was a small and, many of my boy friends would think, an unattractive collection. But in the collection was the "Spectator," in reading which Daniel unconsciously did something towards forming a desirable style of his own. He was fond of poetry, and at an early age could repeat many of the psalms and hymns of Dr. Watts.

There was another poem which so impressed him that he learned to repeat the whole of it. This was Pope's "Essay on Man," a poem which I fear is going out of fashion, which is certainly a pity, for apart from its literary merits it contains a great deal of sensible advice as to the conduct of life. As it is not of so much importance how much we read as how thoroughly, and how much we remember, there is reason to think that Daniel got more benefit from his four books than most of the boys of to-day from their multitude of books.

Once, however, Daniel's literary enthusiasm came near having serious consequences. A new almanac had been received, and as usual each of the months was provided with a couplet of poetry. After going to bed Daniel and Ezekiel got into a dispute about the couplet at the head of the April page, and in order to ascertain which was correct Dan got out of bed, went down stairs, and groped his way to the kitchen, where he lighted a candle and went in search of the almanac. He found it, and on referring to it ascertained that Ezekiel was right. His eagerness made him careless, and an unlucky spark from the candle set some cotton clothes on fire. The house would have been consumed but for the exertions and presence of mind of his father. It may be a comfort to some of my careless young readers to learn that so great a man as Daniel Webster occasionally got into mischief when he was a boy.

Somewhere about this time a young lawyer, Mr. Thomas W. Thompson, came to Daniel's native town and set up an office.

As he was obliged to be absent at times, and yet did not wish to close his office, he proposed to Daniel to sit in his office and receive callers in his absence. Though boys do not generally take kindly to confinement, the office contained one attraction for the boy in a collection of books, probably of a miscellaneous character such as a young man is likely to pick up.

Daniel's time was not otherwise occupied, for he had no service to render, except to stay in the office and inform callers when Mr. Thompson would be back, and he was therefore at liberty to make use of the books. He made a selection unusual for a boy. There was an old Latin grammar, which the young lawyer had probably used himself in his preparatory course. This book Daniel selected, and began to study by himself. His employer offered to hear him recite in it, and soon had occasion to be surprised at the strong and retentive memory of his office boy. Probably none of the law books attracted the future lawyer. It would have been surprising if they had.

"Judge Webster," said Thompson, on meeting the father of his young employee, "Dan will make a fine scholar if he has the chance."

"I think the boy has ability."

"He certainly has. He ought to go to college."

Judge Webster shook his head.

"I should like it above all things," he said, "but I can't see my way clear. I am a poor man, as you know, and it would cost a great deal of money to carry Dan through college even after he were prepared."

This was true, and the young lawyer was unprepared with any suggestion as to how the difficult matter was to be arranged. But Judge Webster did not forget the conversation. He was considering what could be done towards giving his promising son an education. He was willing to sacrifice his comfort, even, if thereby he could give him a good start in life.

Finally he made up his mind to start him on the way, even if he were obliged to stop short before reaching the desired goal.

Not far away was an institution which has since become famous, Exeter Academy, which has now for a century been doing an important work in preparing boys for our best colleges, and has always maintained a high standard of scholarship. Thither Judge Webster determined to take Daniel, and provide for his expenses by domestic self-denial. It was not till he had fully made up his mind that he announced his determination to the boy.

"Dan," he said one evening, "you must be up early to-morrow."

"Why, father?"

Daniel supposed he was to be set at some farm work.

"We are going to make a journey," answered Judge Webster.

"A journey!" repeated the boy in surprise. "Where are we going?"

"I am going to take you to Exeter, to put you at school there."

The boy listened with breathless interest and delight, mingled perhaps with a little apprehension, for he did not know he would succeed in the untried scenes which awaited him.

"Won't it be expensive, father?" he asked after a pause, for he knew well his father's circumstances, and was unusually considerate for a boy.

"Yes, my son, but I look to you to improve your time, so that I may find my investment a wise one."

"How are we to go, father?"

"On horseback."

Dan was a little puzzled, not knowing whether he and his father were to ride on one horse or not, as was a frequent custom at that time. It would have been hard upon any horse, for the judge was a man of weight, and the boy though light would have considerably increased the burden.

The next morning Daniel's curiosity was gratified. In front of the farmhouse stood two horses, one belonging to his father, the other filled out with a side-saddle.

"Is that horse for me?" asked Daniel in surprise.

"Yes, my son."

"What do I want of a side-saddle? I am not a lady."

"Neighbor —— is sending the horse to Exeter for the use of a lady who is to return here. I agreed to take charge of it, and it happens just right, as you can use it."

"I don't know how I can get along with it. It will look strange for me to be riding on a lady's saddle."

"If a lady can ride on it probably you can."

So Dan and his father set out on their journey from the quiet country town to Exeter, the boy mounted on a lady's horse. When in his later life he had occasion to refer to this journey, Mr. Webster recalled with great merriment the figure he must have cut as he rode meekly behind his father.

No doubt as they rode along father and son conversed together about the important step which had been taken. Judge Webster already had formed the plan of sending Daniel to college, after he should have completed a course of preparation at Exeter, but upon this part of his plan he did not think it best yet to speak to his son, very probably because he had not yet made up his mind as to whether his circumstances would allow him to incur so heavy an expense.

"My son," said the father gravely, "I hope you will improve to the utmost the advantages I am securing for you. You must remember how much depends upon yourself. A boy's future is largely in his own hands."

"Yes, father, I will do the best I can."

"Mr. Thompson thinks you can make a good scholar."

"I will try, father."

"I shall have no money to leave you, Daniel, but I hope to give you an education, which is better than a fortune."

How would the father have been gratified if he could have foreseen the brilliant future in store for the boy of fourteen who was about to take his first important step in life.

CHAPTER V.

DANIEL AT EXETER ACADEMY.

THE principal of Exeter Academy at that time was Benjamin Abbot, LL.D., a man of high repute in letters as well as in the educational field. He was a man of dignified presence, who exacted and received deference not only from his pupils but from all with whom he came in contact.

"Dr. Abbot," said Judge Webster, when the two were admitted to his presence, "I have brought my son Daniel to study in your institution, if you find him qualified."

The dignified principal turned towards the bashful boy, and said, "What is your age, sir?"

"Fourteen," answered Daniel.

"I will examine you first in reading. Take this Bible, my lad, and read that chapter."

It was the twenty-second chapter of St. Luke's Gospel, and was very well adapted as a test of the boy's ability in reading.

Now if there was anything Dan could do well

it was this. He never could remember the time when he could not read. Probably he had learned from his mother, and his first text-book was the Bible. He was endowed with reverence, and his grave, sonorous voice was especially well fitted for sacred reading.

The boy took the book and commenced the task prescribed. Usually a few verses are considered sufficient, but in this case the dignified listener became absorbed in the boy's reading, and he listened, half forgetful of the object he had in view. It is a good deal to say that he actually enjoyed it. He had seldom listened to a voice at once so rich, deep and sonorous as belonged to this young boy of fourteen. Daniel, too, forgot that he was on trial, and read with his whole soul intent upon the words before him.

When he had completed the chapter Dr. Abbot said, abruptly, "You are qualified to enter this institution."

This was all the examination which in his case was required.

It was no common school that Daniel had entered, as is shown by the list of eminent men who have gone forth from it. George Bancroft, Edward Everett, Alexander H. Everett, Lewis Cass, Levi Woodbury, John E. Palfrey and others received here the first rudiments of their classical education, and all of them looked back with affection to their Alma Mater. But without derogating from the fame of any of these eminent men, it may surely be said that in Daniel Webster not only Exeter but Dartmouth College boasts its greatest alumnus.

Daniel soon vindicated the good judgment of Dr. Abbot in admitting him as a pupil. As to the manner in which he improved the advantages which his father's self-denial had secured to him, I quote the testimony of Dr. Tefft in his interesting life of Webster:

"During the nine months of his stay at Exeter he accomplished as much for himself, according to every account, as most young gentlemen could have accomplished in two years. When he left he had as thoroughly mastered grammar, arithmetic, geography and rhetoric, as the majority of college graduates usually have done after a full collegiate course. He had also made rapid progress in the study of the Latin language. Dr. Abbot, fully appreciating the capacity of his most remarkable pupil, did not tie him down to the ordinary routine of study, nor compel him to lag behind with the other pupils, but gave him free scope and a loose rein, that he might do his utmost; and the venerable preceptor, after the lapse of more than half a century, during all which time he continued to be a teacher, declared on a public occasion that Daniel Webster's equal in the power of amassing knowledge he had never seen, and never expected to see again.

"It is not enough to say of him, according to Dr. Abbot's description of him at this time, that he had a quick perception and a memory of great tenacity and strength. He did not seem barely to read and remember, as other people do. He appeared, rather, to grasp the thoughts and facts given by his author with a peculiar force, to incorporate them into his mental being, and thus make them a part of himself. It is said of Sir Isaac Newton, after reading for the first time the geometry of Euclid, and on being asked what he thought of it, that he knew it all before. He understood geometry, it seems, by intuition, or by a perception so rapid that it seems like intuition; but it was also true of the great astronomer that he had great difficulty in remembering even his own calculations after he had gone through with them. Daniel Webster, on the other hand, though endowed with a very extraordinary quickness of insight, worked harder for his knowledge than did Newton; but when once he had gained a point, or learned a fact, it remained with him, a part of his own essence, forever afterwards. His mind was also wonderfully fertile. A single truth, which, with most boys of his age, would have remained a single truth, in him became at once a starting-point for a remarkable series of ideas, original and striking, growing up out of the seed sown by that mighty power of reflection, in which no youth of his years, probably, was ever his superior."

At that time an assistant in the school was Joseph S. Buckminster, who later became an eminent preacher in Boston, and died while yet a young man. He was very young at the time, a mere boy, yet such were his attainments, and such was the confidence reposed in him by his old teachers, that he was selected to fill the position of tutor. He it was who first directed the studies of the new scholar, and encouraged the bashful boy to do his best. In after life Webster never displayed timidity or awkwardness; but, fresh from the farm, thrown among a hundred boys, most of whom were better dressed and more used to society than he, he felt at times awkward and distrustful. One thing he found it hard to do was to declaim. This is certainly singular, considering how he excelled in reading, and considering moreover what an orator he afterwards became.

It was not because he did not try. He committed more than one piece to memory, and recited it to himself out loud in the solitude of his own room, but when the time came to get up and declaim it before the teacher and his schoolmates he was obliged to give it up. Here is his own account of it:

"Many a piece did I commit to memory, and rehearse in my own room over and over again; but when the day came, when the school collected, when my name was called, and I saw all eyes turned upon my seat, I could not raise myself from it. Sometimes the masters frowned, sometimes they smiled. Mr. Buckminster always pressed and entreated with the most winning kindness that I would venture only *once;* but I could not command sufficient resolution, and when the occasion was over I went home and wept tears of bitter mortification."

This is certainly encouraging for bashful boys. Here was a man who became one of the greatest orators—perhaps *the* greatest—and yet as a boy he made an ignominious failure in the very department in which he afterwards excelled. It is a lesson for parents also. Don't too hastily conclude that your boys are dunces, and destined to failure, because they develop late, or are hindered from making a creditable figure by timidity or nervous self-consciousness.

In this connection I am tempted to repeat an

anecdote of Sir Walter Scott. It was not till comparatively late that he discovered his poetical ability. It is related of him that when already a young man he was rowing with a friend on a Scotch lake, when they mutually challenged each other to produce a few lines of poetry. Both made the trial, and both failed. Thereupon Scott said good-humoredly to his companion, "It's clear neither of us was cut out for a poet." Yet within ten years appeared the first of those Border poems which thrilled the hearts of his countrymen, and have lent a charm to the hills and lakes of Scotland which they will never lose.

Daniel remained nine months at Exeter. Though he did not win reputation as a declaimer, he made his mark as a scholar. When he was approaching the end of his first term the usher said one day, "Webster, you may stop a few minutes after school; I wish to speak to you."

Daniel stopped, wondering whether in any way he had incurred censure.

When they were alone the usher said, "The term is nearly over. Are you coming back next term?"

Daniel hesitated. He enjoyed the advantages which the school afforded, but his feelings had been hurt at times by the looks of amusement directed at his rustic manners and ill-fitting garments.

The usher noticed his hesitation, and said, "You are doing yourself great credit. You are a better scholar than any in your class. If you come back next term I shall put you into a higher class."

These encouraging words made the boy resolve to return, and regardless of ridicule pursue with diligence the path which had been marked out for him.

It would be rather interesting to read the thoughts of Daniel's schoolmates when years afterwards they saw the boy whom they had ridiculed moving forward with rapid strides to the foremost place in the councils of state, as well as in the legal profession.

I am tempted to insert here, on the authority of an Exeter correspondent of the Chicago *Advance*, an anecdote of Daniel at this period which will interest my young readers:

"When Daniel Webster's father found that his son was not robust enough to make a successful farmer, he sent him to Exeter to prepare for college, and found a home for him among a number of other students in the family of 'old Squire Clifford,' as we of a younger generation had always heard him called. Daniel had up to this time led only the secular life of a country farmer's boy, and, though the New Hampshire farmers have sent out many heroes as firm and true as the granite rocks in the pasture, there cannot be among the hard and homely work which such a life implies the little finenesses of manner which good society demands. Daniel was one of these diamonds of the first water, but was still in the rough, and needed some cutting and polishing to fit him to shine in the great world in which he was to figure so conspicuously.

"None saw this more clearly than the sensible old Squire. The boy had one habit at table of which the Squire saw it would be a kindness to cure him. When not using his knife and fork he was accustomed to hold them upright in his fists, on either side of his plate. Daniel was a bashful boy of very delicate feelings, and the Squire feared to wound him by speaking to him directly on the subject. So he called aside one of the other students with whom he had been longer acquainted, and told him his dilemma. 'Now,' said he, 'I want you this noon at the table to hold up your knife and fork as Daniel does. I will speak to you about it, and we will see if the boy does not take a hint for himself.'

"The young man consented to be the capegoat for his fellow-student, and several times during the meal planted his fists on the table, with his knife and fork as straight as if he had received orders to present arms. The Squire drew his attention to his position, courteously begged his pardon for speaking of the matter, and added a few kind words on the importance of young men correcting such little habits before going out into the world. The student thanked him for his interest and advice, and promised reform, and Daniel's knife and fork were never from that day seen elevated at table."

CHAPTER VI.

PREPARING FOR COLLEGE.

AFTER nine months spent at Exeter Daniel was withdrawn by his father, not from any dissatisfaction with the school or with the pupil's progress, but probably for economical reasons. Judge Webster was a poor man, and though the charges at Exeter at that time were very moderate they were a heavy draft upon the good father's purse. But Dan was not taken back to farm-work. He was allowed to continue his classical studies, but under different auspices.

In the town of Boscawan, only six miles off, the minister, Rev. Samuel Wood, was noted for his success in preparing boys for college. His charges, too, were wonderfully low. For board and instruction he only charged one dollar per week, which leads us to infer either that provisions were very cheap, or that boys had less appetite than is the case now. At any rate, the low price was a great inducement to Dan's father.

"Dan," he said, soon after the boy came, "do you wish to continue your studies?"

"Yes, father, if you are willing."

"I am not only willing but desirous that you should do so. I intend to place you with Rev. Mr. Wood, of Boscawen."

Daniel knew of Mr. Wood's reputation as a teacher, and the prospect did not displease him.

Still his father had not announced the plan he had in view for him.

One cold winter day, when the snow lay deep on the ground, Judge Webster and Dan started for the house of his future teacher. As they were ascending a hill slowly through deep snows the Judge, who had for some time been silent, said, "Dan, I may as well tell you what plan I have in view for you. I shall ask Mr. Wood to prepare you for college, and I will let you enter at Dartmouth as soon as you are ready."

Daniel could not speak for emotion. He knew what a sacrifice it would involve for his father with his straitened means to carry through such a plan as that, and his heart was full. As he himself says, "A warm glow ran all over me, and I laid my head on my father's shoulder and wept."

I am afraid that some boys—possibly some of my young readers—have received a similar announcement from their fathers with quite different feelings.

We are to imagine Dan, then, an inmate of the minister's family, pursuing his studies with success, but with less of formal restraint than when he was a pupil at Exeter. Indeed I shall not attempt to conceal the fact that occasionally Dan's love of sport, and particularly of fishing, drew him away from his studies, and led him to incur the good doctor's remonstrances.

One day after a reprimand, which was tempered, however, by a compliment to his natural abilities, Daniel determined to surprise his teacher.

The task assigned him to prepare was one hundred lines of Virgil, a long lesson, as many boys would think. Daniel did not go to bed, but spent all night in poring over his book.

The next day, when the hour for recitation came, Dan recited his lesson with fluency and correctness.

"Very well," said Dr. Wood, preparing to close the book.

"But, doctor, I have a few more lines that I can recite."

"Very well," said Mr. Wood, supposing that Dan might have read twenty-five or thirty lines more. But the boy kept on till he had completed a second hundred.

"Really, Dan, I compliment you on your industry," said his teacher, again about to close the book.

"But," said Dan, "I have studied further."

"Very remarkable," said the minister in surprise; "well, let us have them."

Dan rolled off another hundred lines, which he appeared to know quite as well as the previous two hundred.

"You are a smart boy!" said the doctor approvingly, and not without a feeling of relief, for it is rather tedious to listen critically to the translation of three hundred lines.

"But," said Dan, "I am not through yet."

"Pray how much have you read?" asked Dr. Wood in amazement.

"I can recite five hundred more if you like," said Dan, his eyes twinkling with enjoyment at the doctor's surprise.

"I think that will do for to-day," said Dr. Wood. "I don't think I shall have time to hear them now. You may have the rest of the day for pigeon shooting."

Indeed Dan was always fond of sport, and not particularly fond of farm-work. My boy reader may like to read an anecdote of this time, which I will give in the very words in which Daniel told it to some friends at a later day.

While at Dr. Wood's, "my father sent for me

in haying time to help him, and put me into a field to turn hay, and left me. It was pretty lonely there, and, after working some time, I found it very dull; and, as I knew my father was gone away, I walked home, and asked my sister Sally if she did not want to go and pick some whortleberries. She said yes. So I went and got some horses, and put a side-saddle on one, and we set off. We did not get home till it was pretty late, and I soon went to bed. When my father came home he asked my mother where I was, and what I had been about. She told him. The next morning when I awoke I saw all the clothes I had brought from Dr. Wood's tied up in a small bundle again. When I saw my father he asked me how I liked haying. I told him I found it 'pretty dull and lonesome yesterday.' 'Well,' said he, 'I believe you may as well go back to Dr. Wood's.' So I took my bundle under my arm, and on my way I met Thomas W. Thompson, a lawyer in Salisbury; he laughed very heartily when he saw me. 'So,' said he, 'your farming is over, is it?'"

It will occur to my readers that, as Judge Webster was struggling so earnestly to give Dan an education, it would have been more considerate for the boy to have remained at his task, and so saved his father the trouble of finishing it. However, it is not my intention to present the boy as in all respects a model, though it is certain that he appreciated and was thoroughly grateful for his father's self-sacrificing devotion.

On one occasion Dan was set to mowing. He did not succeed very well.

"What is the matter, Dan?" asked his father.

"My scythe does not *hang* well," answered Dan, an answer which will be understood by country boys.

His father took the scythe and tried to remedy the difficulty, but when it was handed back to Dan, it worked no better.

"I think you had better hang it to suit yourself, Dan," said his father.

With a laughing face Dan hung it on the branch of a tree, and turning to his father said, "There, that is just right."

On another occasion Judge Webster, on returning home, questioned the boys as to what they had been doing in his absence.

"What have you been doing, Ezekiel?" asked his father.

"Nothing, sir," was the frank reply.

"And you, Daniel, what have you been doing?"

"*Helping Zeke, sir.*"

There is no doubt that Judge Webster was

more indulgent than was usual in that day to
his children, and more particularly to Daniel, of
whose talents he was proud, and of whose future
distinction he may have had in his mind some
faint foreshadowing. This indulgence was increased by Dan's early delicacy of constitution.
At any rate, Daniel had in his father his best
friend, not only kind but judicious, and perhaps
the eminence he afterwards attained was due in
part to the judicious management of the father,
who earnestly sought to give him a good start in
life.

While at Boscawan Dan found another circulating library, and was able to enlarge his reading
and culture. Among the books which it contained was an English translation of Don Quixote, and this seems to have had a powerful
fascination for the boy. "I began to read it," he
says in his autobiography, "and it is literally true
that I never closed my eyes until I had finished
it, nor did I lay it down, so great was the power
of this extraordinary book on my imagination."

Meanwhile Daniel was making rapid progress
in his classical studies. He studied fitfully perhaps, but nevertheless rapidly. In the summer
of 1797, at the age of fifteen, he was pronounced
ready to enter college. His acquisitions were by
no means extensive, for in those days colleges

were content with a scantier supply of preparatory knowledge than now. In the ancient languages he had read the first six books of Virgil's Æneid, Cicero's four Orations against Catiline, a little Greek grammar, and the four Evangelists of the Greek Testament. In mathematics he had some knowledge of arithmetic, but knew nothing of algebra or geometry. He had read a considerable number of books, however, enough to give him a literary taste, but he was by no means a prodigy of learning. Yet, slender as were his acquirements, his school life was at an end, and the doors of Dartmouth College opened to receive its most distinguished son.

CHAPTER VII.

DANIEL'S COLLEGE LIFE.

It is an important point in a boy's life when he enters college. He leaves home, in most cases, and, to a greater extent than ever before, he is trusted to order his own life and rely upon his own judgment. It is a trying ordeal, and many fail to pass through it creditably. A student who has plenty of money is in greater danger of wasting his time from the enlarged opportunities of enjoyment which money can buy. From this danger, at least, Daniel was free. His father found it hard enough to pay his ordinary expenses, and it is hardly likely that the boy ever had much spare money to spend on pleasure.

Besides, though only fifteen, Daniel already possessed a gravity and earnestness not often to be found in much older students. These, however, were blended with a humor and love of fun which contributed to make him an agreeable companion for his fellow-students.

Daniel's development was not rapid. The oak tree grows steadily, but in rapidity of growth it is eclipsed by many trees of less importance. The great powers which our hero exhibited in after life did not at once make themselves manifest. He did not at once take his place proudly at the head of his class. This is shown by the fact that at the Sophomore exhibition neither of the two principal appointments was assigned to him. Notwithstanding this, it may safely be asserted that his time was well spent. In this connection I am sure my young readers will be interested in reading the testimony of Professor Shortliff.

"Mr. Webster, while in college," writes the professor, "was remarkable for his steady habits, his intense application to study, and his punctual attendance upon all the prescribed exercises. I know not that he was absent from a recitation, or from morning and evening prayers in the chapel, or from public worship on the Sabbath; and I doubt if ever a smile was seen upon his face during any religious exercise. He was always in his place, and with a decorum suited to it. He had no collision with any one, nor appeared to enter into the concerns of others, but emphatically minded his own business. But, as steady as the sun, he pursued with intense application the great object for which he came to college."

This is certainly high praise, and I am afraid such words could hardly be said with truth of the majority of the college students of to-day. Conscientious devotion to duty is often set down by college students as indicating a lack of proper spirit, and the punctilious scholar is often stigmatized as a toady, who is trying to curry favor with the Faculty. Daniel, however, understood very well how important to his future success was his improvement of the advantages which his father's self-sacrifice had purchased for him. Judge Webster was obliged to mortgage his house and farm to meet the expenses incurred by Daniel's education, and he would indeed have been most reprehensible if he had not constantly borne this in mind.

To go into details, Daniel's favorite studies were the Latin and Greek classics. He was but slenderly versed in these languages when he entered college, and the college course was not as advanced as it is at Dartmouth to-day. The first year, and part of the second, was devoted to authors and studies which now receive attention before entrance. For instance, the Freshman class went on with the Seventh Book of the Æneid and with the remainder of the Greek Testament, arithmetic was continued, and algebra was begun. While he was not below the average in mathematics, Daniel certainly did not excel in that department. It is related of Charles Sumner that he made strenuous efforts to become a good mathematical scholar in spite of, perhaps because of, his conscious distaste for that important branch, but without marked success. General reading and composition always attracted him, and he was probably one of the best read students at the time in college. He devoted his leisure hours to extensive readings in poetry, history and criticism. His powerful and retentive memory made this voluntary course of especial value, and years later there were times when he was able to make happy and striking quotations from authors he had not read since his college life.

It is quite certain that Daniel at this time had no path marked out for his future life, yet he probably could not have made a more profitable preparation for that which actually lay before him than that which he was unconsciously making. The history of England and of his own country especially interested him, not alone the history of outward events, but the constitutional history. From the age of eight he had been familiar with the Constitution of the United States, read for the first time as printed on the cheap cotton handkerchief, of which mention has already been made. He never ceased to study it, and he well deserved the title sometimes given him of Expounder and Defender of the Constitution.

At that time, as at present, it was the custom for the students to form societies, in which debates and other literary exercises were the principal features of the periodical meetings. Towards the middle of his college course Daniel joined "The United Fraternity," then the leading society in college. He had long since overcome the diffidence which at Exeter prevented him from participating in the exercise of declamation. In the society he became distinguished both as a writer and debater, and ere long ranked in the general estimation as the best writer and speaker in college. So far as he exhibited precocity in anything he showed it in these two branches. His method of preparation, for he always prepared himself when he proposed to speak, is described by a classmate as follows: "He was accustomed to arrange his thoughts in his mind in his room or his private walks, and to put them upon paper just before the exercise would be called for. When he was required to speak at two o'clock, he would frequently begin to write after dinner, and when the bell rang he would fold his paper, put it in his pocket and go in, and speak with great ease. In his movements he was rather slow and deliberate, except when his feelings were aroused; then his whole soul would kindle into a flame."

As this was the formative period when young Webster's intellectual character was taking shape; as, moreover, he was still a boy in years, no older than many who will read this book, I add another tribute to his industry in college and the ability which he displayed. It is from a letter written by Hon. Henry Hubbard to Prof. Sanborn.

"I entered the Freshman class in 1799," writes Mr. Hubbard, "at the early age of fourteen. I was two years in college with Mr. Webster. When I first went to Hanover I found his reputation already established as the most remarkable young man in the college. He was, I believe, so decidedly beyond any one else that no other student of his class was ever spoken of as *second* to him. I was led, very soon, to appreciate most highly his scholarship and attainments. As a student his acquisitions seemed to me to be very extensive. Every subject appeared to contribute something to his intellectual stores. He acquired knowledge with remarkable facility. He seemed to grasp the meaning and substance of a book almost by intuition. Others toiled long and patiently for that which he acquired at a glance.

"As a scholar, I should say that he was then

distinguished for the uncommon extent of his knowledge, and for the ease with which he acquired it. But I should say that I was more impressed by his eloquence and power as a speaker, before the society of which we were both members, than by his other qualifications, however superior to others. There was a completeness and fullness in his views, and a force and expressiveness in his manner of presenting them, which no other student possessed. We used to listen to him with the deepest interest and respect, and no one thought of equaling the vigor and glow of his eloquence. The oration which he delivered before the United Fraternity on the day of his graduation is, I think, now among the records of that society. Whoever will read it at this late day, and bring to mind the appearance of the author, his manner and power, during its delivery, cannot fail to admit that I have said no more of his eloquence than I was warranted in saying. The students, and those who knew him best and judged him most impartially, felt that no one connected with the college deserved to be compared with him at the time he received his first degree. His habits and moral character were entirely unimpeachable. I never heard them questioned during our college acquaintance."

After this testimony I am certainly justified in

holding up Daniel Webster, during his college life, as a fit model for all young men who at this day are placed in similar circumstances and pursuing a similar course.

CHAPTER VIII.

DANIEL RECEIVES SOME VALUABLE ADVICE.

PETER HARVEY, in his interesting volume of "Reminiscences of Daniel Webster," relates many incidents for which he was indebted to the free and friendly communications of Mr. Webster himself. One of these I will transfer to my pages, as it will be likely to amuse my young readers. I can do no better than quote it without alteration from Mr. Harvey's book.

"Mr. Webster was once telling me about a plain-spoken neighbor of his father, whose sons were schoolmates of his own. The neighbor had moved into the neighborhood of Hanover, where he had opened a little clearing, and had settled upon a piece of comparatively barren land. After Daniel had been in college several months his father said to him,

"'John Hanson is away up there somewhere. I should like to know how he is getting along. I think you had better find him out, and go and see him.'

"So Daniel inquired about, and soon found out pretty nearly where Hanson lived.

"'One Saturday afternoon,' related Mr. Webster, 'I thought I would trudge up there through the woods, and spend Sunday with my old friends. After a long, tedious walk I began to think I should never find the place; but I finally did, and when I got there I was pretty well tired out with climbing, jumping over logs, and so on. The family were not less delighted than surprised to see me, but they were as poor as Job's cat. They were reduced to the last extreme of poverty, and their house contained but one apartment, with a rude partition to make two rooms.

"'I saw how matters were; but it was too late to go back, and they seemed really glad to see me. They confessed to me that they had not even a cow, or any potatoes. The only thing they had to eat was a bundle of green grass and a little hog's lard, and they actually subsisted on this grass fried in the hog's fat. But it was not so bad after all. They fried up a great platter of it, and I made my supper and breakfast off it. About a year and a half afterwards, just before graduating, I thought that, before leaving Hanover, I would go and pay another visit to the Hansons. I found that they had improved somewhat, for they now had a cow and plenty of plain, homely fare. I spent the night there, and was about to leave the next morning, when Hanson said to me,

"'"Well, Daniel, you are about to graduate. You've got through college, and have got college larnin', and now, what are you going to do with it?"

"'I told him I had not decided on a profession.

"'"Well," said he, "you are a good boy; your father was a kind man to me, and was always kind to the poor. I should like to do a kind turn to him and his. You've got through college, and people that go through college either become ministers, or doctors, or lawyers. As for bein' a minister I would never think of doin' that; they never get paid anything. Doctorin' is a miserable profession; they live upon other people's ailin's, are up nights, and have no peace. And as for bein' a lawyer, I would never propose that to anybody. Now," said he, "Daniel, I'll tell you what! You are a boy of parts; you understand this book-larnin', and you are bright. I knew a man who had college larnin' down in Rye, where I lived when I was a boy. That man was a conjurer; he could tell by consultin' his books and study if a man had lost his cow where she was. That was a great thing, and if people lost anything, they would think nothin' of payin' three or four dollars to a man like that, so as to find their property. There is not a conjurer within a hundred miles of this place; and you are a bright boy, and have got this college larnin'. The best thing you can do, Daniel, is to study that, and *be a conjurer!*"'"

We can imagine the serious, earnest tone in which this advice was given, and we may easily suppose that Daniel found it hard not to laugh when the climax was reached. We can hardly imagine the advice to have been taken. If, in place of Daniel Webster, the great lawyer, and the defender of the Constitution, we had Daniel Webster, the famous conjurer, it would be a ludicrous transformation. There are few persons who do not consider themselves qualified to give advice, but when my young readers are advised about the serious business of life, let them consider whether the advice comes from one who is qualified by wisdom and good judgment to give it.

CHAPTER IX.

BROTHERLY LOVE.

DANIEL's path seemed to lie plain before him. He was a college student, receiving and using such advantages as Dartmouth could give him. At nineteen he would be a graduate, and well qualified to commence a professional course. So far as he was concerned Daniel felt that he had reason to congratulate himself. But there was another for whom he began to feel solicitude.

Ezekiel Webster was nearly two years older than Daniel, and like him possessed uncommon natural gifts. A strong affection had united the two brothers from their earliest years. There was no reason, apart from Judge Webster's poverty, why Ezekiel, as well as his younger brother, should not be allowed a college education. But the father hesitated long before he ventured to offer Daniel the education which he longed to give him, and to raise the necessary money was obliged to mortgage his humble house. His plan for Ezekiel was that he should remain at home and carry on the farm. As he grew older, and hard work had made him in his own words "old before his time," he felt that it would be a relief to have a son like Ezekiel to take the burden from his shoulders, and keep up the farm. But Ezekiel scarcely more than Daniel had a vocation for farming. He too had a thirst for learning, and felt that a farmer's life would be uncongenial. It is natural that he should have felt dissatisfied with his prospects, and that the claims of Duty which he recognized should nevertheless have seemed to him difficult to obey.

Such was the state of feeling when Daniel came home on a vacation. To him Ezekiel revealed his thoughts and inward struggles.

"I ought to stay, Daniel," he said; "now that you are away father needs me more than ever, but I can't bear the idea of growing up in ignorance, with no work more elevating than working on the farm."

Daniel was touched. He could see how unequal their lots were likely to be. While he might be a successful lawyer, his favorite brother, whose talents he considered to equal his own, would have to toil on the barren acres of their paternal farm.

"I can't bear the idea, either, Zeke," he answered. "You are sacrificing yourself to me. Father has mortgaged the farm to pay my expenses, and you are working to pay it."

"If but one of us can have an education, Dan, I am glad that you are that one."

"But, Zeke, you are as smart as I, nay, smarter, and ought to have the same advantages."

"It cannot be, Daniel. I know that well enough. If I could be spared to leave home I should like to go out West. In a new part of the country I should have a better chance of getting on than here. Here on our barren little farm there is no chance to do better than get a bare living."

"I wish you could go to college too. Isn't there some way of managing it?"

"I have thought of it many times, but I see no way," answered Ezekiel despondently.

"May I mention the subject to father, Zeke?"

"It would only trouble him, and after all it would do no good."

All night long the two brothers talked the matter over, and finally Zeke gave his consent to Dan's broaching the subject to their father. The result I will give in Daniel's words.

"I ventured on the negotiation, and it was carried, as other things often are, by the earnest and sanguine manner of youth. I told him [Judge Webster] that I was unhappy at my brother's prospects. For myself I saw my way to knowledge, respectability and self-protection; but as to him, all looked the other way; that I would keep school, and get along as well as I could, be more than four years in getting through college, if necessary, provided he also could be sent to study. He said at once he lived but for his children; that he had but little, and on that little he put no value, except so far as it might be useful to them; that to carry us both through college would take all he was worth; that, for himself, he was willing to run the risk, but that this was a serious matter to our mother and two unmarried sisters; that we must settle the matter with them, and if their consent was obtained, he would trust to Providence, and get along as well as he could."

So the matter was referred to Mrs. Webster, and she showed a devotion equal to that exhibited by her husband. Though she knew that the education of both of her boys would take the balance of their little property, she never hesitated. "I will trust the boys," she answered promptly.

Her confidence was not misplaced. She lived long enough to rejoice in the success of both sons, and to find a happy and comfortable home with

Ezekiel. Nothing in the life of Daniel Webster is more beautiful than the devotion of the parents to their children, and the mutual affection which existed between them.

CHAPTER X.

THE TWO BROTHERS.

EZEKIEL was worthy of the sacrifices his parents made for him. If he was not the equal of Daniel in ability, he was still remarkable, and in time reached high rank as a lawyer in his native State. He was a man grown, and nearly a man in years, when his new plan of life was formed. He was close upon twenty years of age, a young man of striking appearance, "an improved edition of his father in form and features," but thus far he had had only such educational advantages as were afforded by the common schools of his native town. But a small academy had been established in Salisbury, and of this he enrolled himself as a pupil. He remained here for two years, beginning the Latin grammar, for it was necessary, notwithstanding his age, to begin at the lowest round of the ladder.

From the academy he went to reside with Dr. Wood, and under him completed his preparatory studies. The good minister was justly proud of having trained two such pupils as Daniel and Ezekiel Webster.

Between the two brothers the natural relations of older and younger seemed to be reversed Ezekiel looked up to Daniel, though the latter was two years his junior, and asked his advice, but Daniel never assumed the superiority which his elder brother was so ready to concede. Here is an extract from one of his letters: "You tell me that you have difficulties to encounter which I know nothing of. What do you mean, Ezekiel? Do you mean to flatter? That don't become you; or, do you think you are inferior to me in natural advantages? If so, be assured you greatly mistake. Therefore, for the future say in your letters to me, 'I am superior to you in natural endowments; I will know more in one year than you do now, and more in six than you ever will.' I should not resent this language. I should be very well pleased in hearing it; but be assured, as mighty as you are your great puissance shall never insure you a victory without a contest."

It will be seen how warm and free from jealousy were the relations between these two brothers. The spectacle is particularly pleasing because in so many families we find the case so different. Alienation, jealousy and strife are too often found. When brothers band together, cherishing a community of plans and interests, as in the case of the well-known publishers, the Harper brothers, their chance of a large and enduring success is much greater than it would be if all pulled in different directions.

Ezekiel entered college just as Daniel, his younger brother, was leaving it. As he was destined to be associated with Daniel afterwards, my young readers may like to know how he succeeded in college. I quote, from the private correspondence of Daniel Webster, a letter written by Rev. George T. Chapman touching this point:

"All my recollections of Ezekiel Webster are of a gratifying character. In the Senior year we occupied rooms opposite to each other, in a building directly north of the college. I am therefore able to state, from intimate personal acquaintance, that he was altogether exemplary in his habits and faithful in his studies. He had no enemies, and all were happy to be numbered in the list of his friends.

"Owing to his absence in teaching school, no part was assigned him at Commencement. But I have no doubt he stood high in the estimation of the college Faculty; and although I should hesitate to pronounce him the first scholar in his class, it would be doing injustice to his memory to say that he was excelled by either of those who received the highest college honors on the day of our graduation. It has been recently stated that he was particularly distinguished for his knowledge of Greek; but I cannot now recall the circumstance to mind, nor, in fact, make any discrimination as to relative proficiency in the several branches of study. He was deficient in none. He was good in all. Such at least is my recollection of the reputation he enjoyed. After leaving college, from all that I have heard, he obtained a greater degree of eminence in the eye of the public than any of his classmates; and when I revert to college days, after the lapse of almost half a century, all my recollections of what he then was cause me to feel no surprise at the subsequent elevation which he attained."

I think I am justified in saying that Ezekiel was worthy of his relationship to Daniel, though he was overshadowed by the more brilliant talents and success of his younger brother. It is to be considered, however, that he was cut off in the midst of his career, before he had attained the age of fifty, and we cannot tell what might have been had he lived twenty years longer.

But we must not forget that it is the life and the gradual development of Daniel's powers that we are studying. My young readers will probably be surprised to learn that in college he was known as a poet, and appears to have written verse on many occasions with considerable facility. That he would ever have achieved eminence in this class of composition no one will claim, but as the productions of such a youth his verses merit notice. That my readers may judge for themselves, I will quote entire a letter in rhyme written by Daniel a little before he attained the age of seventeen. It was addressed to his friend, George Herbert:

"DARTMOUTH COLLEGE, Dec. 20, 1798.

"Dear George, I go. I leave the friend I love.
Long since 'twas written in the books above.
But what, good God! I leave thee, do I say?
The thought distracts my soul, and fills me with dismay.
But Heaven decreed it, let me not repine;
I go; but, George, my heart is knit with thine.
In vain old Time shall all his forces prove
To tear my heart from the dear friend I love;
Should you be distant far as Afric's sand,
By Fancy pictured, you'd be near at hand.
This shall console my thoughts till time shall end:
Though George be absent, George is still my friend.
But other friends I leave; it wounds my heart
To leave a Gilman, Conkey and a Clark;
But hope through the sad thought my soul shall bear:
Bereft of hope I'd sink in dark despair.
When Phœbus a few courses shall have run,
And e'er old Aries shall receive the sun.

I shall return, nor more shall fear the day
That from my friends shall take poor me away.
Oh then roll on, ye lagging wheels of time,
Roll on the hours; till then, dear George, I'm thine.
"D. W."

Verse-writing was but an episode, an occasional diversion, with Daniel, and when he entered upon his professional life he found little time to devote to it. I will therefore cite but one other specimen of his college productions in this line. It was written shortly after his eighteenth birthday, and was appended to a letter written to his intimate friend, Mr. Bingham.

It runs thus:

"SYLVARUMQUE POTENS DIANA. A FABLE.

"Bright Phœbus long all rival suns outshone,
And rode triumphant on his splendid throne.
When first he waked the blushes of the dawn,
And spread his beauties o'er the flowery lawn,
The yielding stars quick hastened from the sky,
Nor moon dare longer with his glories vie;
He reigned supreme, and decked in roseate light
Beamed his full splendors on the astonished sight.
At length on earth behold a damsel rise,
Whose growing beauties charmed the wondering skies!
As forth she walked to breathe the balmy air,
And view the beauties of the gay parterre,
Her radiant glories drowned the blaze of day,
And through all nature shot a brighter ray.

Old Phœbus saw—and blushed—now forced to own
That with superior worth the damsel shone.
Graced with his name he bade her ever shine,
And in his rival owned a form divine!"

One trait of the young college student I must refer to, because young men at that stage in their mental training are too apt to be marked by a self-sufficient and not altogether agreeable opinion of their own powers. Notwithstanding his great abilities Daniel was always modest, and disposed to under rather than overestimate himself. Shortly after his graduation he took occasion to express himself thus, in speaking to some friends:

"The opinion of my scholarship was a mistaken one. It was overestimated. I will explain what I mean. Many other students read more than I did, and knew more than I did. But so much as I read I made my own. When a half hour, or an hour at most, had elapsed, I closed my book and thought over what I had read. If there was anything peculiarly interesting or striking in the passage I endeavored to recall it and lay it up in my memory, and commonly could effect my object. Then if, in debate or conversation afterwards, any subject came up on which I had read something, I could talk very easily so far as I had read, and then I was very careful to stop.

Thus greater credit was given me for extensive and accurate knowledge than I really possessed."

It may be remarked generally that men of great abilities are more likely to be modest than third-rate men, who are very much afraid that they will not be rated as high as they should be. There are indeed exceptions, and those of a conspicuous character. The poet Wordsworth had a comfortable consciousness of his superiority to his contemporaries, and on one occasion, when he was asked if he had read the poems of such a one (a prominent poet), he answered, "I never read any poetry except my own."

It is a safe rule to let the world pronounce you great before you call attention to your own greatness.

CHAPTER XI.

DANIEL AS AN ORATOR.

THE four years spent in college generally bear an important relation to the future success or non-success of the student. It is the formative period with most young men, that is, it is the time when the habits are formed which are to continue through life. Let us inquire, then, what did Daniel Webster's college course do for him?

We cannot claim that his attainments at graduation were equal to those of the most proficient graduates of our colleges to-day. The curriculum at Dartmouth, and indeed at all colleges, was more limited and elementary than at present. Daniel was a good Greek and Latin scholar for his advantages, but those were not great. He did, however, pay special attention to philosophical studies, and to the law of nations. He took an interest in current politics, as may be gathered from letters written in his college days, and was unconsciously preparing himself for the office of a statesman.

He paid special attention also to oratory. No longer shrinking from speaking before his classmates, he voluntarily composed the pieces he declaimed, and took an active part besides in the debating society. I am sure my young reader will like to know how Daniel wrote at this time, and will like to compare the oratory of the college student with that of the future statesman. I shall, therefore, quote from a Fourth of July oration, which he delivered by invitation to the citizens and students at the age of eighteen. As in a boy's features we trace a general likeness to his mature manhood, so I think we may trace a likeness in passages of this early effort to the speeches he made in the fullness of his fame.

This is the opening of the address:

"*Countrymen, Brethren and Fathers:* We are now assembled to celebrate an anniversary, ever to be held in dear remembrance by the sons of freedom. Nothing less than the birth of a nation, nothing less than the emancipation of three millions of people from the degrading chains of foreign bondage is the event we commemorate.

"Twenty-four years have this day elapsed since these United States first raised the standard of liberty, and echoed the shouts of independence. Those of you who were then reaping the iron harvest of the martial field, whose bosoms then palpitated for the honor of America, will at this time experience a renewal of all that fervent patriotism, of all those indescribable emotions, which then agitated your breasts. As for us, who were either then unborn, or not far enough advanced beyond the threshold of existence to engage in the grand conflict for liberty, we now most cordially unite with you to greet the return of this joyous anniversary, to welcome the return of the day that gave us freedom, and to hail the rising glories of our country."

Further on he paints the hardships and distresses through which the colonists had passed:

"We behold a feeble band of colonists engaged in the arduous undertaking of a new settlement in the wilds of North America. Their civil liberty being mutilated, and the enjoyment of their religious sentiments denied them in the land that gave them birth, they braved the dangers of the then almost unnavigated ocean, and sought on the other side of the globe an asylum from the iron grasp of tyranny and the more intolerable scourge of ecclesiastical persecution.

"But gloomy indeed was the prospect when arrived on this side of the Atlantic.

"Scattered in detachments along a coast immensely extensive, at a distance of more than three thousand miles from their friends on the eastern continent, they were exposed to all those evils, and encountered or experienced all those difficulties, to which human nature seemed liable. Destitute of convenient habitations, the inclemencies of the seasons harassed them, the midnight beasts of prey howled terribly around them, and the more portentous yell of savage fury incessantly assailed them. But the same undiminished confidence in Almighty God, which prompted the first settlers of the country to forsake the unfriendly climes of Europe, still supported them under all their calamities, and inspired them with fortitude almost divine. Having a glorious issue to their labors now in prospect, they cheerfully endured the rigors of the climate, pursued the savage beast to his remotest haunt, and stood undismayed in the dismal hour of Indian battle."

Passing on to the Revolutionary struggle the young orator refers to "our brethren attacked and slaughtered at Lexington, our property plundered and destroyed at Concord," to "the spiral flames of burning Charlestown," and proceeds as follows:

"Indelibly impressed on our memories still lives the dismal scene of Bunker's awful mount, the grand theater of New England bravery, where slaughter stalked grimly triumphant, where relentless Britain saw her soldiers, the unhappy instruments of despotism, fallen in heaps beneath the nervous arm of injured freemen!

"There the great Warren fought, and there, alas! he fell. Valuing his life only as it enabled him to serve his country, he freely resigned himself a willing martyr in the cause of liberty, and now lies encircled in the arms of glory.

> "'Peace to the patriot's shade—let no rude blast
> Disturb the willow that nods o'er his tomb;
> Let orphan tears bedew his sacred urn,
> And fame's proud trump proclaim the hero's name
> Far as the circuit of the spheres extends!'

"But, haughty Albion, thy reign shall soon be over. Thou shalt triumph no longer; thy empire already reels and totters; thy laurel even now begins to wither and thy fame to decay. Thou hast at length aroused the indignation of an insulted people; thy oppressions they deem no longer tolerable.

"The Fourth Day of July, 1776, has now arrived, and America, manfully springing from the torturing fangs of the British lion, now rises majestic in the pride of her sovereignty, and bids her eagle elevate his wings! The solemn Declaration of Independence is now pronounced, amidst crowds of admiring citizens, by the supreme council of the nation, and received with the unbounded plaudits of a grateful people! That was the hour when heroism was proved— when the souls of men were tried!

"It was then, ye venerable patriots," there were some Revolutionary soldiers present—"it was then you lifted the indignant arm, and unitedly swore to be free! Despising such toys as subjugated empires, you then knew no middle fortune between liberty and death. Firmly relying on the protection of Heaven, unwarped in the resolution you had taken, you then undaunted met, engaged, defeated the gigantic power of Britain, and rode triumphant over the aggressions of your enemies!

"Trenton, Princeton, Bennington and Saratoga were the successive theaters of your victories, and the utmost bounds of creation are the limits of your fame! The sacred fire of freedom, then enkindled in your breasts, shall be perpetuated through the long descent of future ages, and burn with undiminished fervor in the bosoms of millions yet unborn!"

Further on we find the following passage:

"The great drama is now completed; our independence is now acknowledged, and the hopes of our enemies are blasted forever. Columbia is now sealed in the forum of nations, and the empires of the world are amazed at the effulgence of her glory.

"Thus, friends and citizens, did the kind hand of an overruling Providence conduct us, through toils, fatigues and dangers, to independence and peace. If piety be the rational exercise of the human soul, if religion be not a chimera, and if the vestiges of heavenly assistance are clearly traced in those events which mark the annals of our nation, it becomes us on this day, in consideration of the great things which have been done for us, to render the tribute of unfeigned thanks to that God who superintends the universe, and holds aloft the scale that weighs the destinies of nations."

The oration was a long one, and touched a variety of topics, but the extracts already given will convey a good idea of its excellencies and defects. My college readers will understand me when I say that the style is sophomoric and ambitious, but these faults may be pardoned in a youth of eighteen. The tone is elevated, it is marked by gravity and earnestness, the sentiments are just, there is evidence of thought, and, on the whole, we may regard the oration as a hopeful promise of the future. The magniloquence gave place in time to a weighty simplicity, in which every word told, and not one could be spared. It was rather remarkable that so young a man should have been selected to deliver such an address in Hanover, and indicates that Daniel had by this time acquired reputation as a public speaker.

This was not the only occasion on which he was selected to speak in public. When a classmate, a general favorite, died, young Webster was unanimously selected to deliver an address of commemoration. He is said to have spoken with a fervor and eloquence which deeply stirred the hearts of the large audience that had assembled to hear him. "During the delivery the fall of a pin could have been heard at any moment; a dense audience were carried entirely away, and kept spellbound by the magic of his voice and manner; and when he sat down, he left a thousand people weeping real tears over a heartfel sorrow. It is reported that there was not a dry eye in all the vast congregation which the event and the fame of the orator had brought together."

CHAPTER XII.

STUDYING LAW.

DANIEL had now successfully accomplished the first object of his ambition. He was a college graduate. Though not the first scholar in his class he was very near the head, and probably in general culture stood first. There was a little misunderstanding which led to his declining to appear at Commencement. His friends desired him to deliver the valedictory, but the Faculty selected another, and Daniel remained silent. There is a report that he tore up his diploma in anger and disgust in presence of his classmates, saying, "My industry may make me a great man, but this miserable parchment cannot." Had this story been true it would have done Daniel little credit. George Ticknor Curtis, who has written the most elaborate and trustworthy memoir of Webster states emphatically that there is no foundation for this story. Even if not entirely satisfied with the treatment he received at that time, Daniel's loyalty to his Alma Mater was never doubted.

And now the world was before the young graduate. What was he to do?

His thoughts had long been fixed upon the legal profession. This was no proof of a special fitness for it, for at least half of the young men who graduate from our colleges make the same choice. But with Daniel the choice was a more serious one, for he very well knew that he could not afford to make a mistake here. Poverty was still his hard taskmaster, and he leaned beneath its dark shadow.

My young reader will remember that at the age of fourteen Daniel officiated as office-boy for a young lawyer in his native town—Thomas W. Thompson. Now a college graduate of nineteen, he re-entered the same office as a law student. Mr. Thompson was a man of ability. He was a graduate of Harvard, where also he had filled the position of tutor. While the boy was obtaining an education at Dartmouth, Thompson was establishing a lucrative law practice. He became in time prominent in State politics, and finally went to Congress. It will be seen, therefore, that Daniel made a good choice, and that Mr. Thompson was something more than an obscure country lawyer.

It is a little significant that the first law books which the young student read related to the law of nations. He read also standard literary works, and gave his leisure hours to hunting and fishing, the last of which was always a favorite sport with him. He gained some insight into the practical business of a law office. The reader will be amused at a humorous account of the manner in which he was employed during a temporary absence of his legal preceptor and a fellow-student.

"I have made some few writs," he says, "and am now about to bring an action of trespass for breaking a violin. The owner of the violin was at a husking, where

'His jarring concord, and his discord dulcet,'

made the girls skip over the husks as nimbly as Virgil's Camilla over the tops of the corn, till an old surly creature caught his fiddle and broke it against the wall. For the sake of having plump witnesses the plaintiff will summons all the girls to attend the trial at Concord."

Here is another extract from a letter to the same friend which will amuse: "I thank you for your receipt for greasing boots. Have this afternoon to ride to the South Road, and in truth my boots admit not only water, but peas and gravelstones. I wish I had better ones. As for 'his new friend, tobacco,' he is like most of that name has made me twice sick, and is now dismissed.

"Heighho! a man wants a remedy against his neighbor, whose lips were found damage-feasant on his—the plaintiff's—wife's cheek! What is to be done? But you have not read the law against kissing. I will write for advice and direction to Barrister Fuller."

So the young man appeared to be enjoying himself while pursuing his studies, and would probably have wished nothing better than to have gone on till he was prepared for admission to the bar on his own account. But there was a serious obstacle. His good father had well nigh exhausted his means in carrying Daniel through college, and Ezekiel through his preparatory studies, and was now very much straitened for money. It was felt to be time for Daniel to help him. He, therefore, "thought it his duty to suffer some delay in his profession for the sake of serving his elder brother," by seeking employment outside.

As a general thing when a college graduate is pressed by hard necessity, he turns his attention to the task of teaching, and such was the case with Daniel. Fortunately he soon found employment. From Fryeburg, Maine, there came to him an invitation to take charge of the academy there, and the young man accepted it. He was to be paid the munificent salary of three hundred and fifty dollars per year, and he felt that the offer was too dazzling to be rejected.

CHAPTER XIII.

HOW DANIEL WENT TO FRYEBURG.

WHEN a young college graduate of to-day sets out for the scene of his dignified labors, he packs his trunk and buying a ticket for the station nearest the favored spot where he is to impart knowledge, takes his seat in a comfortable car, and is whirled rapidly to his destination.

Not thus did Daniel go. Railroads had not been heard of, and no stages made the trip. He therefore purchased a horse for twenty-four dollars, deposited his limited wardrobe and a few books in his saddle-bags, and like a scholastic Don Quixote set out by the shortest path across the country for Fryeburg. In due time he arrived, and the trustees of the academy congratulated themselves on having secured Daniel Webster, A.B., as their preceptor. How much more would they have congratulated themselves could they have foreseen the future of the young teacher.

Let me pause here to describe the appearance

of the young man, as his friends of that time depict him. He was tall and thin (he weighed but one hundred and twenty pounds, which was certainly light weight for a man not far from six feet in height), with a thin face, high cheek bones, but bright, dark, penetrating eyes, which alone were sufficient to make him remarkable. He had not wholly overcome the early delicacy which had led his friends to select him as the scholar of the family, because he was not strong enough to labor on the farm. His habitual expression was grave and earnest, though, as we have seen, he had inherited, and always retained, a genial humor from his father.

Three hundred and fifty dollars seems a small salary, but Daniel probably didn't regard it with disdain Expenses were small, as we are told that the current rate of board was but two dollars per week, less than a third of his income. Then his earnings were increased by a lucky circumstance.

Young Webster found a home in the family of James Osgood, Esq., registrar of deeds for the county of Oxford. Mr. Osgood did not propose to do the work himself, but was authorized to get it done.

One evening soon after the advent of his new boarder, the registrar said, "Mr. Webster, have you a mind to increase your income?"

"I should be exceedingly glad to do so, sir," answered the young man, his face brightening with hopeful expectation.

"You are aware that I hold the position of registrar of deeds for the county. It is my duty to see that all deeds are properly recorded?"

"Yes, sir."

"This work I do not care to do myself, having sufficient other work to occupy my time. How would you like to undertake it in the evening? It would not interfere with your school duties."

"I am not a very good penman," said the young man doubtfully.

"Handsome penmanship is not required. It is sufficient if the deeds are copied in a plain, legible hand, and this may be attained by effort."

"How much compensation would be allowed?"

"I receive two shillings and threepence for each deed recorded. I will allow you one shilling and sixpence, and you can average two deeds in an evening. What do you say?"

One shilling and sixpence was twenty-five cents. Two deeds therefore would bring the young teacher fifty cents, and four evenings' work, therefore, would pay his board, and leave him his salary clear. This was a tempting inducement though it would involve dry and tedious labor.

"I will accept," said Daniel promptly.

"Then you can begin at once," said Mr. Osgood, well satisfied.

It was a hard way of earning money, but money was very much needed. So, after the fatigues of the day, when supper was over, Daniel sat down to record dry deeds. The curious visitor to Fryeburg can still see two volumes of deeds, a large part of them in Daniel Webster's handwriting. Though not a good writer, he forced himself to write well, and in his autobiography he says, "The ache is not yet out of my fingers, for nothing has ever been so laborious to me as writing, when under the necessity of writing a good hand."

I may be permitted to call the attention of my young readers to this point—that what he had undertaken to do he did well, although it was a task far from congenial. A young man or boy who observes this rule is likely to succeed in the end: Whatever you have to do do as well as you can.

CHAPTER XIV.

THE PRECEPTOR OF FRYEBURG ACADEMY.

It may be supposed that between his school in the daytime and his duties as copyist in the evening, Daniel found his time pretty well occupied. As we know, he was not drawn to the teacher's office by any special love of that honorable vocation, but simply by the pecuniary emolument. But, though this was the case, he discharged his duties with conscientious fidelity, and made himself a favorite both among his pupils and in the village, where the new preceptor was, as is usual, a person of importance.

He was accustomed to open and close the school with extemporaneous prayer, and those who remember the deep solemnity of manner which he could command at will will readily believe that this exercise was made impressive by the young teacher.

No stories have been handed down of insubordination among his pupils. If there had been any, it would speedily have been quelled by the preceptor, whose demeanor was naturally dignified.

It is remarkable how many of our great men have spent a portion of their early lives at the teacher's desk. Gen. Garfield had an unusually extensive and varied experience as teacher, and would have passed through life very happily if he had never withdrawn from the school-room. Daniel Webster had not his special aptitude for it, but was nevertheless very fairly successful. One qualification, as we learn from the testimony of a pupil, was his "remarkable equanimity of temper." The vexations of the school-room are neither few nor far between, but none of them were able to bring a frown to young Webster's brow. Calmly he met and conquered all difficulties that came in his way, and secured the confidence and respect of his scholars.

The young man also impressed his pupils and friends as a man of competent scholarship. Hon. Samuel Fessenden, of Portland, writes: "The first I ever knew of Daniel Webster was immediately after he left college, and was employed by my father, the secretary of the Trustees of Fryeburg Academy, to become the principal instructor in that institution. He was not, when he commenced, twenty years old. I heard no one complain that his scholarship was not adequate to the duty he had assumed. On the contrary, I heard the Rev. Dr. Nathaniel Porter, of Conway, and my father, the Rev. William Fessenden, of Fryeburg, both of whom were good scholars, and the former, Rev. Dr. Porter, a very great man, say that Daniel Webster was a very good scholar for his years. He did, while at Fryeburg, exhibit traits of talent and genius which drew from these two divines, and from other professional gentlemen, unqualified praise of his powers of mind. I remember very distinctly hearing my father remark that if Mr. Webster should live, and have health, and pursue a straightforward course of industry and virtue, he would become one of the greatest men this country had produced."

When it is remembered that the young man of whom this prediction was made was at the time an obscure teacher, in an obscure town, in what was then a frontier settlement, we must infer that he exhibited remarkable ability, and gave hints of a reserved power not yet called into action.

In spite of his engrossing employments, the young man found time to enlarge his general culture by various reading. Nor did he neglect his professional studies, but continued the reading of Blackstone's Commentaries. It is remarkable that with all this hard work he found time for society. Dr. Osgood, the registrar's son, says: "He was usually serious, but often facetious and pleasant. He was an agreeable companion, and eminently social with all who shared his friendship. He was greatly beloved by all who knew him. His habits were strictly abstemious, and he neither took wine nor strong drink. He was punctual in his attendance upon public worship, and ever opened his school with prayer. I never heard him use a profane word, and never saw him lose his temper."

From all that has been said my young readers will see that Daniel was beginning life in the right way. It seems to me that at this period he was a model who may be safely copied in all respects. The reverence which he so plainly evinced as a young man for religion he never lost, but to the latest day of his life he yielded to none in his regard for the spirit of Christianity.

Under date of May 18, 1802, Daniel writes to his favorite friend Harvey Bingham, giving some account of matters at Fryeburg. He had just returned from spending a short vacation with his brother at Hanover.

"I arrived here last night," he says; "but must fill this page by relating a little anecdote that happened yesterday. I accidentally fell in

with one of my scholars on his return to the
academy. He was mounted on the ugliest horse
I ever saw or heard of except Sancho Panzas's
pacer. As I had two horses with me, I proposed to
him to ride one of them; he did accordingly, and turned her forward, where her odd appearance, indescribable gait, and frequent stumblings afforded
us constant amusement. At length we approached Saco River, a very wide, deep and rapid
stream, when this satire on the animal creation,
as if to revenge herself on us for our sarcasms,
plunged into the river, then very high by the
freshet, and was wafted down the current like a
bag of oats. I could scarcely sit on my horse for
laughter. I am apt to laugh at the vexations of
my friends. The fellow, who was of my own
age, and my roommate half checked the current by
oaths as big as lobsters, and the old Rosinante, who
was all the while much at her ease, floated up among
the willows far below on the opposite shore."

While Daniel was laboring as teacher and
copyist at Fryeburg, his older brother, Ezekiel,
was pursuing his studies at Dartmouth College,
sustained there mainly by the remittances which
Daniel was able to send him. The chief pleasure
which the younger brother derived from his experience as teacher was, that it gave him the

means of securing for his favorite brother the same advantages which he had himself enjoyed. He cheerfully postponed his plan of professional study in order to discharge this pious duty. Certainly the affection which united these two brothers was very beautiful, and creditable to both. Too often brothers are estranged without good reason, and follow selfishly their own plans, without the desire to help each other. To the end of Ezekiel's life this mutual affection continued, and when he was suddenly removed by death Daniel was deeply affected, and staggered under the blow.

How long was this occupation to continue! How long was the future statesman to devote himself to the comparatively humble duty of inducting country boys into the paths of knowledge?

He had only engaged for two terms, but such was his success that the trustees were not willing to have him go. As an inducement to him to remain they offered to increase his small salary of three hundred and fifty dollars to five or six hundred, with a house to live in, a piece of land to cultivate, and possibly a clerkship of the Common Pleas.

All this may sound very small to us, but to a youth who had been reared in such straitened circumstances as Daniel it seemed like a liberal competence. It required some decision and boldness to reject this certainly for the uncertain prospects of a young lawyer, before whom lay at the first a period of poverty and struggle. Then it must be added that Daniel was modest, and was far from believing that he was endowed with extraordinary talent. It is very probable that more than half the young men who graduate from our law schools to-day have a higher opinion of their abilities than Daniel Webster at the age of twenty. To illustrate his struggles I quote from a letter written at this time.

"What shall I do? Shall I say, 'Yes, gentlemen,' and sit down here to spend my days in a kind of comfortable privacy, or shall I relinquish these prospects, and enter into a profession where my feelings will be constantly harrowed by objects either of dishonesty or misfortune; where my living must be squeezed from penury (for rich folks seldom go to law), and my moral principle be continually at hazard? I agree with you that the law is well calculated to draw forth the powers of the mind, but what are its effects on the heart? are they equally propitious? Does it inspire benevolence and awake tenderness; or does it, by a frequent repetition of wretched objects, blunt sensibility and stifle the still, small voice of mercy?

"The talent with which Heaven has intrusted me is small, very small; yet I feel responsible for the use of it, and am not willing to pervert it to purposes reproachful or unjust, or to hide it, like the slothful servant, in a napkin.

"On the whole, I imagine I shall make one more trial (of the law) in the ensuing autumn. If I prosecute the profession, I pray God to fortify me against its temptations. To the winds I dismiss those light hopes of eminence which ambition inspired and vanity fostered. To be 'honest, to be capable, to be faithful' to my client and my conscience. I believe you, my worthy boy, when you tell me what are your intentions. I have long known and long loved the honesty of your heart. But let us not rely too much on ourselves; let us look to some less fallible guide to direct us among the temptations that surround us."

In a letter written June 4, 1802, Mr. Webster refers to his indecision as to a career.

"Now Hope leans forward on Life's slender line,
Shows me a lawyer, doctor or divine;
Ardent springs forward to the distant goal,
But indecision clogs the eager soul.
Heaven bless my friend, and when he marks his way,
And takes his bearings o'er life's troubled sea,
In that important moment may he find
Choice and his friends and duty all combined."

CHAPTER XV.

THE NEXT TWO YEARS.

THE die was cast! Daniel decided to forego the small but comfortable income insured to him as a teacher, and in accordance with his father's wishes, as well as his own inclination, returned to the study of the law. He resumed his place (September, 1802) in the office of Mr. Thompson, at Salisbury, and there he remained till February or March, 1804. Before leaving Fryeburg, at the request of the citizens he delivered a Fourth of July oration (his second), for which he received from the trustees of the academy a gratuity of five dollars! It was not many years before five hundred dollars would not have been considered too much for such a service from the then obscure teacher.

My young readers would not feel particularly interested in the details of Daniel's professional studies during the eighteen months he spent in the office of Mr. Thompson. From the larger biographies such information may be obtained by law students and those who take an interest therein. I shall content myself by extracting from Mr. Webster's autobiography some account of the manner in which he employed his time.

"I do not know whether I read much during this year and a half besides law books, with two exceptions. I read Hume through, not for the first time; but my principal occupation with books, when not law books, was with the Latin classics. I brought from college a very scanty inheritance of Latin. I now tried to add to it. I made myself familiar with most of Tully's Orations, committed to memory large passages of some of them, read Sallust and Cæsar and Horace. Some of Horace's odes I translated into poor English rhymes; they were printed. I have never seen them since. My brother was a far better English scholar than myself, and, in one of his vacations, we read Juvenal together. But I never mastered his style, so as to read him with ease and pleasure. At this period of my life I passed a great deal of time alone. My amusements were fishing and shooting and riding, and all these were without a companion. I loved this occasional solitude then, and have loved it ever since, and love it still. I like to contemplate nature, and to hold communion, unbroken by the presence of human beings, with 'this universal frame—thus wondrous fair.' I like solitude also, as favorable to thoughts less lofty. I like to let the thoughts go free and indulge excursions. And when *thinking* is to be done, one must, of course, be alone. No man knows himself who does not thus sometimes keep his own company. At a subsequent period of life I have found that my lonely journeys, when following the court on its circuits, have afforded many an edifying day."

It will be seen that young Webster aimed to be something more than a lawyer. Instead of throwing aside his law books when his daily reading was over with a sigh of relief that he could now devote his time to mere enjoyment, he closed them only to open the English and Latin classics, with a view to broaden his culture and qualify himself for something better than a routine lawyer, to whom his profession presents itself only as a means of livelihood. Pressed as he had been, and still was, by the burden of poverty, he never appears to have set before himself as a principal object the emoluments to be gained by legal practice. During his busy years his receipts were indeed very large, but they came to him as a consequence of his large and varied ability, and not because he had specially labored to that end.

I have already mentioned the young man's

modesty. He did not apparently suspect the extent of his own powers, and did not look forward to fill any conspicuous place in his profession. He hoped indeed for "the acquirement of a decent, competent estate, enabling us to treat our friends as they deserve, and to live free from embarrassment." This was the measure of his expectation.

Yet it did occur to him at times that an office in a small country town hardly afforded the facilities for acquiring professional knowledge which it would be desirable to enjoy. Sometimes he hoped that he might be able to finish his studies in Boston, where he would meet with men of large ability, and where the practice of law took a larger range. But if he found it hard work to maintain himself in Salisbury, how could he hope to pay his way in Boston?

But a way was unexpectedly opened to him. Before Ezekiel had completed his college course it was necessary for him to teach in order to fill his exhausted coffers, and by a lucky chance he obtained the charge of a small private school in what is now Kingston Street, Boston. He had eight scholars in Latin and Greek, but found himself unable to do justice to them on account of the long list of branches which he had to teach. He wrote to Daniel, offering him a sum suffi-

cient to pay his board, if he would assume the
charge of these pupils. This would require but
an hour and a half daily, and would leave the law
student ample time to prosecute his studies.

It may readily be supposed that Daniel did not
decline this offer. It was an experiment, perhaps, but it was worth trying. So he packed up
his clothes and repaired to Boston, where he
joined his brother, whom he arranged to assist in
his duties. Now the relations of the brothers
were again reversed, and it was the elder who
took his turn in helping along the younger. The
most eminent of the pupils thus coming under
the instruction of Daniel Webster was Edward
Everett, worthy as an orator to be named with his
master. Webster, Everett, Choate! Nine out
of ten, if called upon to name the three most renowned orators of New England, would single
out these names, and it will indeed be a fortunate
age that can boast three who can equal them.
Among the pupils of Ezekiel Webster was George
Ticknor, another eminent man who will need no
introduction to my readers.

Daniel had entered a new and auspicious period of study and opportunity. He had gained a
foothold in Boston. How was he best to improve
his residence? What great lawyer would open
his office to the young New Hampshire student?

Among the most eminent citizens and lawyers of Boston at that time was Christopher Gore. He had served the American Government at home and abroad, as district attorney for Massachusetts, and as a commissioner to England under Jay's Treaty, for the settlement of claims brought by citizens of the United States for spoliation by British cruisers during the war of the French Revolution. A higher honor was in store for him, since in 1809 he was elected Governor of Massachusetts by the Federal party. In 1804, when young Webster arrived in Boston, he was in practice as a lawyer, his specialty being commercial law.

Daniel learned that Mr. Gore had no clerk, and ambition led him to apply for the situation. He did not know any near friend of the distinguished lawyer, but a young man, whose acquaintance with him was nearly as slight as his, undertook to introduce him.

When the two young men entered the office, Daniel, according to his own account, was shockingly embarrassed. But Mr. Gore, with his old-fashioned courtesy, speedily put at him at ease. The rest of the interview we will let Mr. Webster tell for himself.

"I had the grace to begin with an unaffected apology; told him my position was very awkward, my appearance there very like an intrusion, and that, if I expected anything but a civil dismission, it was only founded in his known kindness and generosity of character. I was from the country, I said; had studied law for two years; had come to Boston to study a year more; had some respectable acquaintances in New Hampshire, not unknown to him, but had no introduction; that I had heard he had no clerk; thought it possible he would receive one; that I came to Boston to work, not to play; was most desirous, on all accounts, to be his pupil; and all I ventured to ask at present was, that he would keep a place for me in his office till I could write to New Hampshire for proper letters, showing me worthy of it."

This speech Daniel delivered fluently, having carefully considered what he intended to say.

Mr. Gore heard him with encouraging good nature, and kindly invited the young visitor to sit down.

"I do not mean to fill my office with clerks," he said, "but am willing to receive one or two, and will consider what you have said."

He inquired what gentlemen of his acquaintance knew Daniel and his father, and in reply Daniel mentioned several, among others Mr. Peabody, who was Mr. Gore's classmate.

A pleasant conversation continued for a few minutes, and Daniel rose to go.

"My young friend," said Mr. Gore, "you look as if you might be trusted. You say you came to study and not to waste time. I will take you at your word. You may as well hang up your hat at once. Go into the other room, take your book and sit down to reading it, and write at your convenience to New Hampshire for your letters."

Daniel could hardly credit his good fortune in this prompt assent to his wishes. He felt that he had made an auspicious beginning in Boston, and made "a good stride onward" in securing admission to such an office.

CHAPTER XVI.

A GREAT TEMPTATION.

Our young student could not have been more favorably situated for study, and we may well believe that he made the best use of his advantages. I shall not describe his course at length, or in detail, but confine myself to such personal details as are likely to interest my reader.

In November a rare pleasure awaited him. A gentleman of means, Mr. Taylor Baldwin, who had some occasion for his services, engaged him to accompany him on a leisurely journey in parts of New England and New York, not only defraying his expenses, but recompensing him liberally. I can do no better than quote the young man's description of it in a letter to his friend Bingham, dated Jan. 2d, 1805 :

"Figure to yourself a large room in the third story of a brick building, in the center of Boston, a sea-coal fire, and a most enormous writing-table with half a cord of books on it. Then figure further to yourself your most obedient, with his back to the fire, and his face to the table, writing by candle-light, and you will precisely see a 'happy fellow.' There now is a famous dash at description! Now let me try my talent at narration.

"Well, then, on the fifth day of November, being election day, at just twenty-seven minutes and a half past twelve, I left Mrs. Whitwell's, Court Street, Boston, and on the twenty-eighth day of the same month, at one o'clock P.M., arrived at the same Mrs. Whitwell's, in the same Court Street. You can easily determine from the above account where I went!! If, however, you should be puzzled, I will tell you to Albany. Yes, James, I have even been to Albany. I cannot now tell you why, nor for what, but it was in a hackney coach, with a pair of nimble trotters, a smart coachman before, and a footman on horseback behind. There's style for you! Moreover, I had my friend at my elbow. . . . . My expenses were all amply paid, and on my return I put my hand in my pocket, and found one hundred and twenty dear delightfuls! Is not that good luck? And these dear delightfuls were, 'pon honor, all my own, yes, every dog of 'em. Now don't you think I would jump to go to Albany again! But to be serious, I really went to Albany, in November, with a gentleman of this town, for which I received the above reward; and I'm so proud to have a dollar of my own I was determined to tell you of it. Of my journey and all that I saw and heard I cannot give you a particular account now."

The journey above mentioned was through Springfield to Albany, thence down to Hudson, returning by way of Hartford and Providence to Boston. Taken by rail it would not be much of a journey, but traveling by easy stages across the country, it must have been full of enjoyment to a young man wholly new to journeys of any kind.

Daniel's description of Albany in a letter to his brother is an amusing one.

"Albany is no despicable place. To be sure it is irregular and without form. Its houses are generally old and poor-looking—its streets are rather dirty—but there are many exceptions. A part of the town is very high, overlooking the river in a very pleasant manner, and affording many fine seats. Some handsome buildings ornament the town. The Dutch Reformed Church and the new State Bank would not disgrace State Street (Boston). Here are all sorts of people, both Greek and Jew, Englishman and Dutchman, Negro and Indian. Almost everybody speaks English occasionally, though I have heard them speak among themselves in a *lingo* which I never learned even at the Indian Charity School. The river here is half a mile wide, that is, I should think so; and, if I think wrong, you must look at Dr. Morse and correct me."

The cosmopolitan character of Albany nearly eighty years since, when it probably contained not over five thousand inhabitants, is certainly rather amazing, and I can conceive the modern Albanian reading the description given above with considerable surprise. But Daniel was at an age and in a state of inexperience in which everything new is wonderful, and he certainly saw everything under very pleasant circumstances.

From a letter written by his sister it appears that the young law student was paid seven dollars a day for his company by his rich and eccentric companion, who, if he lived to know of Webster's eminence, probably concluded that the price was by no means exorbitant.

In the letter of Sally Webster, already referred to, there is a passage which will amuse my young readers. "Before I have finished my nonsense I must tell you that our neighbors opposite the door fought a duel the other day, one with the gridiron, the other with the candlestick. The female, however, came off victorious, and he, with all speed, ran here with some lint andrum, to be applied immediately, for he was bleeding to death with a wound in his head caused by the gridiron."

It is evident that if the women of New Hampshire were not strong-minded, there were some who were strong-armed, and calculated to strike terror in an average husband.

Meanwhile how were things going at the early home of the future statesman in New Hampshire? Judge Webster no doubt experienced satisfaction in knowing that the two sons for whom he had hoped so much, and sacrificed so much, were now possessors of a collegiate education, and in a fair way to make their own way in the world. But he was not without his anxieties. To obtain that education he had been obliged to mortgage his small estate for nearly all it was worth. He was sixty-five years of age, and a life of labor and exposure had made him old before his time. He could not look for many years more of life, and he might die before his two boys were able to support themselves by their professional labors, without speaking of taking his place at home. But he had been sustained by one hope, which finally seemed in a way of being realized. The clerk of the Court of Common Pleas, of which he was an associate judge, died. Chief Justice Farrar, knowing the family circumstances of his associate, immediately placed the office at his disposal for his son Daniel.

For that day it was a lucrative office, paying much more than a judgeship. The emoluments were fifteen hundred dollars a year, and that would be a competence to a young man brought up like Daniel. It would make life easy to him, and enable him to smooth the pathway of his father, and release the homestead from mortgage.

With glad heart Judge Webster wrote to Daniel of his good fortune, and Daniel on his side was elated. He felt that it would make him independent, that he would pay off the family debt, and assist his brother Ezekiel.

So, full of the good news, he went over to the office in the morning, and with a beaming face acquainted Mr. Gore with the offer he had received, and then waited to receive his congratulations.

"Well, my young friend," said he, "the gentlemen have been very kind to you; I am glad of it. You must thank them for it. Certainly they are very good; you must write them a civil letter. You will write immediately, of course."

"I feel their kindness and liberality very deeply," answered Daniel. "I shall certainly thank them in the best manner I am able, but, as I shall go to Salisbury so soon, I hardly think it is necessary to write."

"Why," said Mr. Gore, seeming greatly surprised, "you surely don't mean to accept it?"

Daniel was astounded. Not to accept such a magnificent proposal! As soon as he could speak he said that he had no thought of anything else but acceptance.

"Well," said Mr. Gore, "you must decide for yourself; but come, sit down, and let us talk it over. The office is worth fifteen hundred a year, you say; well, it never will be worth any more. Ten to one if they find out it is so much the fees will be reduced. You are appointed now by friends; others may fill their places who are of different opinions, and who have friends of their own to provide for. You will lose your place; or, supposing you to retain it, what are you but a clerk for life? And your prospects as a lawyer are good enough to encourage you to go on. Go on, and finish your studies; you are poor enough, but there are greater evils than poverty; live on no man's favor; what bread you do eat let it be the bread of independence; pursue your profession, make yourself useful to your friends, and a little formidable to your enemies, and you have nothing to fear."

Daniel hardly knew what to think or to say. It was presenting the subject from a very different point of view. He had looked forward to this office as a thing greatly to be desired. It had been the height of his ambition, and now his legal instructor, a man whose opinion he greatly valued, told him he must give it up. He was indeed flattered and encouraged by the eminent lawyer's estimate of his talents and prospects, an estimate far beyond any he had formed for himself, for Daniel, as I have already had occasion to say, was modest, and wholly ignorant of the extent of his powers.

It was not that he expected to enjoy a clerkship. He knew he should not, but he had been struggling so long with poverty that the prospect of a competency was most alluring. Besides he was a good son and a good brother. He knew how much his father's mind would be relieved, how he could help his favorite brother, and it seemed very hard to resign such a piece of fortune.

"Go home and think it over," said Mr. Gore, "and come back in the morning, and we will have another talk."

Daniel followed his advice, but passed a sleepless night.

CHAPTER XVII.

DANIEL REFUSES A CLERKSHIP.

THOSE of my readers who have read "The Canal Boy" will remember that before Gen. Garfield graduated from college he too was met by a similar temptation, in the shape of an offer which, if accepted, would have materially changed his course of life, and given him a comfortable obscurity in place of national renown. He was offered a school in Troy, N. Y., with a salary of one hundred and twenty-five dollars per month, while up to that time he had never earned but eighteen dollars per month and board. He declined after a hard struggle, for he too had been reared in poverty and still suffered from it.

And now a similar temptation had come to Daniel Webster.

He went home and thought the matter over. He felt that Mr. Gore's advice was good, but how could he accept it? His father was old and in poor health. He had set his heart on Daniel's accepting this place. A contrary decision would strike him like a thunderbolt. Moreover it would bring him home, and give his father the comfort of his society, as well as pecuniary prosperity.

It seemed a selfish thing to refuse, to show a lack of consideration for his father, and Daniel was a good son. I mention all these things to show that in this turning-point of his career Daniel had a hard decision to make. There was another circumstance to consider—his father was in present need of money.

Finally Daniel made up his mind. If he could borrow a sum of money sufficient to help his father, he would venture to refuse the clerkship.

He went to Mr. Joseph Taylor, a Boston acquaintance, and said to him abruptly, "Mr. Taylor, I want to borrow some money. I will pay you some time or other, but I can't tell exactly when."

"You can have as much as you want," answered Mr. Taylor kindly.

"But," said Daniel, "I want a good deal of money."

"How much?" asked his friend, not seeming alarmed at his rash promise.

"Three or four hundred dollars," was the reply, and this in the eyes of the young law student was a very large sum, though his ideas changed when money came in by thousands from wealthy clients, not many years afterwards.

"You shall have it," said Mr. Taylor, and he counted out the money into the young man's hands.

Daniel was elated with his success. He would not go home empty-handed, and this sum would soften the blow which his determination would bring to his father.

Now to get home and have it over as soon as possible! He hired a seat in a country sleigh which had come down to market, and was on the point of returning, for there was neither railroad nor stage to convey him to his home. It was a crisp winter day, and they glided over the snowy roads for many hours till they were beyond the New Hampshire line. Still mile after mile was traversed till the old home was reached.

Just at sunset Daniel reached his home. Through the window, even before he entered, he saw his father in his little room sitting in his arm-chair. The old man, worn out by a long life of hard labor, seemed very old and thin, but his eyes were as black and bright as ever. Daniel's heart was touched, and he felt that the trial had come. It was no light thing to disappoint such a father.

As he entered the presence of his father Judge Webster looked up with a smile of gladness.

"Well, Daniel, we have got that office for you," he said.

"Yes, father," said Daniel a little nervously. "The gentlemen were very kind. I must go and thank them."

"They gave it to you without my saying a word about it," said Judge Webster complacently.

"I must go and see Judge Farrar, and tell him I am much obliged to him, father."

Still the father suspected nothing of Daniel's intention, though his son treated it more carelessly than he had anticipated. He had thought so much about it and come to look upon it as so desirable that it did not seem to him possible that his son could regard it in any other way, as indeed he would not but for Mr. Gore's advice.

But at last the true meaning of Daniel's indifference flashed upon him, and he looked at him earnestly.

He straightened himself up in his chair, and he regarded him intently.

"Daniel, Daniel," he said, "don't you mean to take that office?"

"No, indeed, father," answered Daniel lightly, though his lightness was assumed, and covered a feeling of anxiety; "I hope I can do much better than that. I mean to use my tongue in the courts, not my pen; to be an actor, not a register of other men's acts. I hope yet, sir, to astonish your honor in your own court by my professional attainments."

Youth is hopeful and ready to take risks; age is conservative and takes little for granted. Judge Webster must have thought his son's decision exceedingly rash. Let me tell the rest of the story in Daniel's words, as indeed I have closely adhered to his version thus far.

"For a moment I thought he was angry. He rocked his chair slightly; a flash went over an eye softened by age, but still as black as jet; but it was gone, and I thought I saw that parental partiality was, after all, a little gratified at this apparent devotion to an honorable profession, and this seeming confidence of success in it. He looked at me for as much as a minute, and then said slowly, 'Well, my son, your mother has always said you would come to something or nothing, she was not sure which; I think you are now about settling that doubt for her.' This he said, and never a word spoke more to me on the subject."

Daniel explained to his father the reasons which had induced him to arrive at the decision he had just expressed, and as an earnest of the good fortune which he anticipated in the career he had chosen he produced the money he had borrowed, and placed it in his father's hands. Probably this satisfied Judge Webster that there were others who had faith in his son's promise, since he could offer no other security for borrowed money. At any rate it softened his disappointment, since it brought him help which he sorely needed.

Daniel stayed at home a week, contributing as such a son might to the happiness of his parents, who, now in the sunset of life, had little to hope for themselves, but lived wholly for their children.

Now he must go back to Boston, for the period of his preparatory studies was drawing to a close, and he was almost to seek immediately admission to the bar.

In March, 1805, he was admitted to practice in the Court of Common Pleas in Boston, the usual motion being made by his friend and teacher, Mr. Gore. This eminent lawyer, according to the custom of that time, accompanied his motion by a brief speech, which was of so complimentary a character that it must have been exceedingly gratifying to the legal neophyte, who stood waiting for the doors to open through which he was to enter into the precincts of a dignified and honorable profession. "It is a well-known tradition," says Mr. George Ticknor Curtis, "that on this occasion Mr. Gore predicted the future eminence of his young friend. What he said has not been preserved; but that he said what Mr. Webster never forgot, that it was distinctly a prediction, and that it excited in him a resolve that it should not go unfulfilled, we have upon his own authority, though he appears to have been unwilling to repeat the words of Mr. Gore's address.

Young Webster, whose career we have thus far followed in detail through the successive stages of his struggle with penury, was now no longer a farmer's boy, but a full-fledged lawyer, of whom eminent men expected much.

Another important question was to be decided. Where should Daniel put up his shingle, and commence the practice of his profession? In Boston the field was larger, and the chances of attaining professional eminence were greater. Many of his friends counseled his remaining in the city. But up in New Hampshire was an old man whose life was nearly over, to whose last days his company would bring solace and comfort. What prospects, however brilliant, could overbalance this consideration? With filial devotion Daniel decided to settle in New Hampshire, in Boscawan, but a few miles from Salisbury, where he could see his father almost daily. Boston could wait, professional opportunities could wait. His father's happiness must not be disregarded. So in the spring of 1805 he became a country lawyer in the same town where he had prepared for college.

Thirteen months later, in April, 1807, his father died.

CHAPTER XVIII.

D. WEBSTER, ATTORNEY.

This was the sign that our young lawyer attached to his office, in the town of Boscawan. The office was humble enough. It was on the second floor of a store, painted red, and the staircase leading to it was on the outside. His office rent was fifteen dollars a year, which certainly could not have been considered an extravagant sum.

Here it was that the future great lawyer commenced practice. Though his fees amounted to but six or seven hundred dollars a year, his practice extended over three counties, Hillsborough, Rockingham and Grafton. We infer from his meager income, though it was ample for his needs in a place where living was so inexpensive, that his clients had no occasion to complain of immoderate charges.

Judge Webster had the satisfaction of hearing his son make one speech in court, but he was so near the end of his earthly pilgrimage that he never heard another, being for the last few months confined within doors. The father listened with satisfaction, and regarded his son's effort as a very creditable one.

Daniel's sole object in establishing himself in an obscure country place was to be near his father, who he knew could not live many years. The end was nearer than he supposed, for he died little more than a year later. It may have been a sacrifice, but probably he lost nothing by it. The quiet seclusion gave him more time for study, and he was laying a broad groundwork for his future fame to rest upon.

It was while he was at Boscawan that he first encountered Mr. Jeremiah Mason, the acknowledged head of the New Hampshire bar. From a foot-note in Curtis's Life, I quote the circumstances as told by Mr. Mason himself.

"I had heard," said Mr. Mason, "that there was a young lawyer up there who was reputed to be a wonderfully able fellow, and was said by the country people to be as black as the ace of spades, but I had never seen him. When they told me that he had prepared evidence for this prosecution (it was a case of forgery, the defendant being a man of respectable position), I thought it well to be careful, especially as the trial was to be conducted by the attorney-general. But when the trial came on the attorney-general was ill, and the prosecutors asked that Webster should be allowed to conduct the case. I assented to this readily, thinking I ought to have an easy time of it, and we were introduced to each other.

"We went at it, and I soon found that I had no light work on my hands. He examined his witnesses and shaped his case with so much skill that I had to exert every faculty I possessed. I got the man off, but it was as hard a day's work as I ever did in my life. There were other transactions behind this one which looked quite as awkward. When the verdict was announced I went up to the dock and whispered to the prisoner, as the sheriff let him out, to be off for Canada, and never to put himself within the reach of that young Webster again. From that time forth I never lost sight of Mr. Webster, and never had but one opinion of his powers."

This is remarkable testimony from the head of the bar to a practitioner so young, who was a mere novice in the profession.

After the death of his father Daniel was still compelled for a time to remain in his country office. His practice was now worth something, and he had it in view to surrender it to his brother Ezekiel, who was now studying law, but had not been admitted to the bar. His father had left some debts, which Daniel voluntarily assumed. In the autumn of 1807 Ezekiel succeeded to the double office of managing the home farm, and carrying on the law business of his younger brother. Then Daniel, feeling that he might safely do so, took down his "shingle," and removed to Portsmouth, where he found a larger field for the exercise of his abilities, where he could gain a higher and more conspicuous position.

His appearance at this time has been thus described by a member of Rev. Dr. Buckminster's family. "Slender, and apparently of delicate organization, his large eyes and narrow brow seemed very predominant above the other features, which were sharply cut, refined and delicate. The paleness of his complexion was heightened by hair as black as the raven's wing."

Daniel soon became intimate with the family of Dr. Buckminster, and from members of this family we learn much that is interesting concerning him. He developed, according to Mr. Lee, a "genial and exceedingly rich humor," which did more to make him popular in society than any of his other diversified gifts. "We young people saw him only rarely in friendly visits. I well remember one afternoon that he came in, when the elders of the family were absent. He sat down by the window, and as now and then an inhabitant of the small town passed through the street, his fancy was caught by their appearance and his imagination excited, and he improvised the most humorous imaginary histories about them, which would have furnished a rich treasure for Dickens, could he have been the delighted listener, instead of the young girl for whose amusement this wealth of invention was extended." Mr. Mason, who appreciated the young man's humor, as well as his professional ability, used to say that " there was never such an actor lost to the stage as he would have made had he chosen to turn his talents in that direction."

Daniel was still fragile, not having yet outgrown his early delicacy. Dr. Buckminster prescribed as a remedy half an hour's wood-sawing before breakfast, with a long two-handed saw, one end of which he held himself. The young lawyer doubtless found this early exercise a good appetizer, qualifying him to do full justice to the breakfast that succeeded.

Within a year of his removal to Portsmouth Mr. Webster took a step most important to his happiness. He was married to Grace Fletcher, daughter of Rev. Elijah Fletcher, of Hopkinton. There is no occasion in a brief biography like this to speak at length of Mrs. Webster. It is sufficient to say that she was qualified by her natural powers and acquired culture to be a sympathizing friend and companion to the husband whom she saw gradually expanding intellectually, and rising higher in reputation, in the twenty years that they lived together.

I have said that Mr. Webster's removal to Portsmouth brought him a wider and more lucrative practice. He still lived plainly, however. His office, though more pretentious than the one at Boscawan, which he hired for fifteen dollars a year, was, according to Mr. Ticknor, "a common, ordinary looking room, with less furniture and more books than common. He had a small inner room, opening from the larger, rather an unusual thing. He lived in a small, modest wooden house, which was burned in the great fire in 1813," a fire by which he lost a valuable library.

Daniel Webster lived in Portsmouth nine years lacking one month. He was in no hurry to remove to the still wider field that was waiting for him in Boston. He says somewhere that these were very happy years. His great powers were gradually expanding. He grew like an oak tree, slowly, but his growth was steady, and the result was massive and majestic. It was not long before he was regarded as one of the most prominent lawyers in his native State, and he was generally matched in important suits with Jeremiah Mason, already referred to as the undisputed head of the bar. Mr. Mason was a remarkable man, not only intellectually but physically. He was a very Titan, almost tall enough to have attracted the attention of Barnum had he lived at a later period. He was six feet seven inches in height, and naturally attracted attention wherever he went—an attention, by the way, which he did not court, and which was embarrassing to him. An amusing story is told of him which I have somewhere read, and will record from memory.

In spite of his great height Mr. Mason did not sit high, having a short body and legs of immense length. One day he was driving in the neighborhood of Portsmouth, when in a narrow road he met a man driving a cart, a stalwart man, inclined to be a bully, who, confident in his strength, was disposed to take advantage of it.

"Turn out!" he said roughly to Mr. Mason.

"My friend," said the lawyer, who was in a light buggy, "I have already given you half the road."

"No, you haven't," answered the other roughly. "At any rate, you must turn out more."

"But I see no justice in that," said the great lawyer mildly.

The mildness of his manner led the bully to think Mr. Mason was afraid of him; so, with an oath, he repeated his demand.

Mr. Mason felt that the matter had gone far enough. He slowly rose in his seat; the country man with astonishment saw what he had supposed to be a man of average height towering into gigantic proportions, and he became alarmed.

"Hold on!" he shouted; "you needn't unroll yourself any more. I'll turn out myself."

This great lawyer, though so often opposed to Webster, was unvaryingly kind to him, and as Daniel himself testifies, was of infinite advantage to him, not only by his friendship, but by the many good lessons he taught him and the example he set him in the commencement of his career.

The young man admired his elder professional brother, and says of him: "If there be in the country a stronger intellect, if there be a mind of more native resources, if there be a vision that sees quicker or sees deeper into whatever is intricate or whatsoever is profound, I must confess I have not known it."

CHAPTER XIX.

DANIEL OVERCOMES A BRAMBLE.

THERE is no doubt that Mr. Webster derived considerable advantage from his association with his elder professional brother. He had adopted a style very common with young men, abounding in large words, and made his sentences longer than were needful. He observed that Mr. Mason, on the other hand, talked to the jury in a plain, conversational way, and cultivated simplicity of diction. Yet he was noted for his success in winning cases. Daniel was sensible enough to correct his fault and prune his too luxuriant style, very much to its improvement.

No admirer of Daniel Webster should fail to read the volume of "Reminiscences" by his life-long friend, Peter Harvey. His confidential relations with his distinguished friend make what he records not only entertaining but trustworthy and valuable. I shall venture to transfer to my pages from Mr. Harvey's volume an account of two cases in which Mr. Webster was engaged during his residence in Portsmouth, with the suggestion that the entire volume will amply repay perusal.

"Among Mr. Webster's reminiscences of his professional career at Portsmouth, and of Jeremiah Mason's connection with it, was one relating to a case in which a man named Bramble was implicated. Matthew Bramble, it appears, was a wealthy resident of Portsmouth, and, as the sequel proved, an unscrupulous man. His social position was good, but a feeling of distrust towards him existed in the community. It seems that Bramble had given to a man named Brown an annuity bond, agreeing to pay him one hundred dollars a year as long as he lived. This was to keep dominant a title to some real estate. Bramble had more than once tried to persuade Brown to take a 'lump' sum of money and cancel the bonds, but this Brown persistently declined to do, and in this he was supported by the advice of his friends. After in vain offering one thousand dollars, Bramble resorted to the following method of getting rid of his obligation. He was accustomed, when he paid the hundred dollars, to indorse it on the bond. The next chance he got, he indorsed, not one hundred dollars, but one thousand dollars, adding 'in full consideration of and canceling this bond.' Brown, who could not read or write, unsuspectingly signed his mark to this indorsement. Bramble then coolly handed him back the bond, and of course said nothing of the matter.

"When the year came round, an altercation took place between them.

"Bramble said, 'I owe you nothing; I paid you a thousand dollars, and it is certified on your bond.'

"Brown was a poor shoemaker, simple-minded, truthful, weak, not capable of coping with this wily scamp. He was friendless, while Bramble was a rich man. Poor Brown did not know what to do. He had convinced his neighbors that he was right. He went to Jeremiah Mason, who told him he was Mr. Bramble's lawyer. Mr. Mason had asked Bramble about the matter, and the latter had showed the bond, and Mr. Mason probably believed him. A friend then advised Brown to go to Mr. Webster; and after hearing his story, Mr. Webster was quite convinced of the truth of Brown's statement. He had no confidence in Bramble. In relating the story, he said to me: 'I knew nothing positively against Bramble, but something impressed me that he was not a man of honor. I was at once satisfied that he had committed this fraud upon Brown, and I told the latter that I would sue Bramble for the annuity. He said he had nothing to give me in payment. I said I wanted nothing. I sent Bramble a letter, and he made his appearance in my office.

"'"I should like to know," he said sharply, "if you are going to take up a case of that kind in Portsmouth? It seems to me you don't know on which side your bread is buttered."

"'"This man has come to me," I replied, "without friends, and has told me a plain, straightforward story, and it sounds as if it were true. It is not a made-up story. I shall pursue this thing, and sue you, unless you settle it."'

"Bramble went to Mr. Mason, who afterwards said to Mr. Webster: 'I think you have made a mistake. Bramble is a man of influence. It can't be that the fellow tells the truth. Bramble would not do such a thing as that.'

"Mr. Webster replied, 'He has done just such a thing as that, and I shall try the suit.'

"So the preliminary steps were taken, and the suit was brought. The case came on at Exeter in the Supreme Court, Judge Smith on the bench. It created great excitement. Bramble's friends were incensed at the charge of forgery, and Brown, too, in his humble way, had his friends. Mr. Webster said: 'I never in my life was more badly prepared for a case. There was no evidence for Brown, and what to do I did not know. But I had begun the suit, and was going to run for luck, perfectly satisfied that I was right. There were Bramble and his friends, with Mason; and poor Brown had only his counsel. And Mason began to sneer a little, saying, "That is a foolish case."

"'Well, a person named Lovejoy was then living in Portsmouth; and when there is a great deal of litigation, as there was in Portsmouth, and many towns in New Hampshire, there will always be one person of a kind not easily described—a shrewd man who is mixed up in all sorts of affairs. Lovejoy was a man of this kind, and was a witness in nearly all the cases ever tried in that section. He was an imperturbable witness, and never could be shaken in his testimony. Call Lovejoy, and he would swear that he was present on such an occasion, and he seemed to live by giving evidence in this way. I was getting a little anxious about the case. I was going to attempt to prove that Brown had been appealed to by Bramble for years to give up his bond, and take a sum of money, and that he had always stoutly refused, that he had no uses for money, and had never been in the receipt of money, and that he could not write, and was easily imposed upon. But although I felt that I was right, I began to fear that I should lose the case.

"'A Portsmouth man who believed in Brown's story came to me just before the case was called, and whispered in my ear, "I saw Lovejoy talking with Bramble just now in the entry, and he took a paper from him."

"'I thanked the man, told him that was a pretty important thing to know, and asked him to say nothing about it.

"'In the course of the trial Mr. Mason called Lovejoy, and he took the oath. He went upon the stand and testified that some eight or ten months before he was in Brown's shop, and that Brown mended his shoes for him. As he was sitting in the shop, he naturally fell into conversation about the bond, and said to Brown, "Bramble wants to get back the bond. Why don't you sell it to him?" "Oh," said Brown, "I have. He wanted me to do it, and as life is uncertain, I thought I might as well take the thousand dollars." He went on to testify that *the said Brown* told him so and so, and when he expressed himself in that way I knew he was being prompted from a written paper. The expression was an unnatural one for a man to use in ordinary conversation. It occurred to me in an instant that Bramble had given Lovejoy a paper, on which was set down what he wanted him to testify. There sat Mason, full of assurance, and for a moment I hesitated. Now, I thought, I will "make a spoon or spoil a horn."

"'I took the pen from behind my ear, drew myself up, and marched outside the bar to the witness stand. "Sir!" I exclaimed to Lovejoy, "give me the paper from which you are testifying!"

"'In an instant he pulled it out of his pocket, but before he had got it quite out he hesitated and attempted to put it back. I seized it in triumph. There was his testimony in Bramble's handwriting! Mr. Mason got up and claimed the protection of the court. Judge Smith inquired the meaning of this proceeding.

"'I said: "Providence protects the innocent when they are friendless. I think I could satisfy the court and my learned brother who, of course, was ignorant of this man's conduct, that I hold in Mr. Bramble's handwriting the testimony of the very respectable witness who is on the stand."

"'The court adjourned, and I had nothing further to do. Mason told his client that he had better settle the affair as quickly as possible. Bramble came to my office, and as he entered I said, "Don't you come in here! I don't want any thieves in my office."

"'"Do whatever you please with me, Mr. Webster," he replied. "I will do whatever you say."

"'"I will do nothing without witnesses. We must arrange this matter."

"'I consulted Mr. Mason, and he said he did not care how I settled it. So I told Bramble that in the first place there must be a new life-bond for one hundred dollars a year, and ample security for its payment, and that he must also pay Brown five hundred dollars and my fees, which I should charge pretty roundly. To all this he assented and thus the case ended.'"

Mr. Webster's professional brothers were very much puzzled to account for his knowing that Lovejoy had the paper in his pocket, and it was not for a long time that he gratified their curiosity and revealed the secret.

My young readers will agree with me that Bramble was a contemptible fellow, and that the young lawyer, in revealing and defeating his meanness, did an important service not only to his client but to the cause of justice, which is often defeated by the very means that should secure it. In many cases lawyers lend themselves to the service of clients whose iniquity they have good reason to suspect. There is no nobler profession than that of law when it is invoked to redress grievances and defeat the designs of the wicked; but, as Mr. Webster himself has said, "The evil is, that an incrersed thirst for money violates everything. We cannot study, because we must pettifog. We learn the low recourses of attorneyism when we should learn the conceptions, the reasonings and the opinions of Cicero and Murray. The love of fame is extinguished, every ardent wish for knowledge repressed, conscience put in jeopardy, and the best feelings of the heart indurated by the mean, money-catching, abominable practices which cover with disgrace a part of the modern practitioners of the law."

CHAPTER XX.

"THE LITTLE BLACK STABLE-BOY."

I am tempted to detail another case in which the young lawyer was able to do an important service to an acquaintance who had known him in his boyhood.

In Grafton County lived a teamster named John Greenough, who was in the habit of making periodical trips to and from Boston with a load of goods. One day, when a mile or two distant from the house of Daniel's father, his wagon was mired, owing to the size of his load and the state of the roads. He found that he could not continue his journey without help, and sent to the house of Judge Webster to borrow a span of horses.

"Dan," said the Judge, "take the horses and help Mr. Greenough out of his trouble."

The boy was roughly dressed like an ordinary farm-boy of that time, his head being surmounted by a ragged straw hat. He at once obeyed his father and gave the teamster the assistance which he so urgently required.

The teamster thanked him for his assistance and drove on, giving little thought to the boy, or dreaming that the time would come when Dan would help him out of a worse scrape.

Years passed and the farm-boy became a lawyer, but Greenough had lost track of him, and supposed he was still at work on his father's farm.

He was a poor man, owning a farm and little else. But a question arose as to his title to the farm. Suit was brought against him, and his whole property was at stake. He secured legal assistance, his lawyer being Moses P. Payson, of Bath. Mr. Payson thought he ought to have help, as the case was an important one, and suggested it to his client. The latter agreed, and Mr. Payson made his selection.

Soon after, in an interview with Mr. Payson, Greenough inquired, "What lawyer have you hired to help you?"

"Mr. Webster," was the reply.

"Webster, Webster!" repeated Greenough; "I don't know any lawyer of that name. Is he from Boston?"

"Oh, no; he came from your neighborhood," was the reply. "It is Daniel Webster, the son of old Ebenezer Webster, of Salisbury."

"What!" exclaimed the teamster in dismay; "that little black stable-boy that once brought me some horses! Then I think we might as well give up the case. Can't you get somebody else?"

"No; the trial cannot be postponed. We must take our chances and make the best of it."

The teamster went home greatly depressed. He remembered the rough looking farm-boy in his rustic garb and old straw hat, and it seemed ridiculous that a good lawyer could have been made out of such unpromising materials. He was not the first man who had been misled by appearances. He was yet to learn that a poor boy may become an able lawyer. Of course the case must go on, but he looked forward to the result with little hope. He would lose his little farm he felt sure, and in his declining years be cast adrift penniless and destitute.

When the day of trial came the teamster was in attendance, but he looked sad and depressed. Mr. Payson made the opening speech, and the trial proceeded. Mr. Webster was to make the closing argument.

When he rose to speak Greenough looked at him with some curiosity. Yes, it was black Dan, a young man now but as swarthy, though better dressed than the boy who had brought him the span of horses to help his wagon out of the mire.

"What can he do?" thought the teamster, not without contempt

Daniel began to speak, and soon warmed to his work. He seemed thoroughly master of the case, and as he proceeded the teamster was surprised, and finally absorbed in his words. He drew nearer and drank in every word that fell from the lips of the "little black stable-boy," as he had recently termed him..

The jury were no less interested, and when the plea closed it was clear how they would render their verdict.

Mr. Payson approached his client, and said with a smile, "Well, Mr. Greenough, what do you think of him now?"

"Think!" exclaimed the teamster. "Why, I think he is an angel sent from heaven to save me from ruin, and my wife and children from misery."

The case was won, and Greenough returned home happy that his little farm would not be taken from him.

Many lawyers aspire to the judicial office as the crowning professional dignity which they may wear with pride. But some of the greatest lawyers are not fitted for that office. They are born advocates, and the more brilliant they are the less, perhaps, do they possess that fair and even judgment which is requisite in a judge. Daniel Webster understood that his talents were not of a judicial character. At a later day (in 1840) he wrote to a friend as follows: "For my own part, I never could be a judge. There never was a time when I would have taken the office of chief justice of the United States or any other judicial station. I believe the truth may be that I have mixed so much study of politics with my study of law that, though I have some respect for myself as an advocate, and some estimate of my knowledge of general principles, yet I am not confident of possessing all the accuracy and precision of knowledge which the bench requires."

For nearly nine years Daniel Webster practiced law in Portsmouth. He could not have selected a more prominent place in New Hampshire; but the time came when he felt that for many reasons he should seek a larger field. One reason, which deservedly carried weight, was, that in a small town his income must necessarily be small. During these years of busy activity he never received in fees more than two thousand dollars a year. Fees were small then compared with what they are now, when lawyers by no means distinguished often charge more for their services in a single case than young Webster's entire yearly income at that time.

When the time came for removal the young lawyer hesitated between Boston, Albany and

New York, but finally decided in favor of the first place. Of his removal we shall have occasion to speak further presently. Before doing so it is well to say that these nine years, though they brought Mr. Webster but little money, did a great deal for him in other ways. He was not employed in any great cases, or any memorable trials, though he and Jeremiah Mason were employed in the most important cases which came before the New Hampshire courts. Generally they were opposed to each other, and in his older professional compeer Daniel found a foeman worthy of his steel. He always had to do his best when Mason was engaged on the other side. That he fully appreciated Mr. Mason's ability is evident from his tribute to him paid in a conversation with another eminent rival, Rufus Choate.

"I have known Jeremiah Mason," he said, "longer than I have known any other eminent man. He was the first man of distinction in the law whom I knew, and when I first became acquainted with him he was in full practice. I knew that generation of lawyers as a younger man knows those who are his superiors in age— by tradition, reputation and hearsay, and by occasionally being present and hearing their efforts. In this way I knew Luther Martin, Edmund Randolph, Goodloe Hart, and all those great lights of the law; and by the way, I think, on the whole, that was an abler bar than the present one—of course with some brilliant exceptions. Of the present bar of the United States I think I am able to form a pretty fair opinion, having an intimate personal knowledge of them in the local and federal courts; and this I can say, that I regard Jeremiah Mason as eminently superior to any other lawyer whom I ever met. I should rather with my own experience (and I have had some pretty tough experience with him) meet them all combined in a case, than to meet him alone and single-handed. He was the keenest lawyer I ever met or read about. If a man had Jeremiah Mason and he did not get his case, no human ingenuity or learning could get it. He drew from a very deep fountain. Yes, I should think he did," added Mr. Webster, smiling, " from his great height."

The young reader will remember that Mr. Mason was six feet seven inches in height.

It is always of great service when a young man is compelled at all times to do his best. Daniel could not oppose such a lawyer as he describes Mr. Mason without calling forth all his resources. It happened, therefore, that the nine years he spent in Portsmouth were by no means wasted, but contributed to develop and enlarge his powers, and provide him with resources which were to be of service to him in the broader and more conspicuous field in which he was soon to exercise his powers.

Furthermore, during these nine years he first entered the arena where he was to gather unfading laurels, and establish his reputation not only as a great lawyer, but one of the foremost statesmen of any age.

I allude to his election to Congress, in which he took his seat for the first time on the 24th of May, 1813, as a Representative from New Hampshire.

CHAPTER XXI.

WHY DANIEL WAS SENT TO CONGRESS.

EVEN in his Sophomore year at college Daniel had taken a considerable interest in public affairs, as might readily be shown by extracts from his private correspondence. This interest continued after he entered upon the practice of the law, but up to the period of his election to Congress he had never filled a public office. It is generally the case with our public men that they serve one or more preliminary terms in one or both branches of the State Legislature, thus obtaining a practical knowledge of parliamentary proceedings. This was not the case with Mr. Webster. His public career would probably have been still further postponed but for the unfortunate state of our relations with England and France for some years preceding the war of 1812.

I can only allude very briefly to the causes which had almost annihilated our commerce and paralyzed our prosperity. Both England and France had been guilty of aggressions upon our commercial rights, and the former government especially had excited indignation by its pretended right to search American vessels for British seamen and deserters. This was intensified by the retaliatory order of Napoleon, issued Dec. 17, 1807, known as the Milan Décrets, in accordance with which every vessel, of whatever nationality, that submitted to be searched, forfeited its neutral character, and even neutral vessels sailing between British ports were declared lawful prizes. Thus America was between two fires, and there seemed to be small chance of escape for any. Moreover, Great Britain interdicted all trade by neutrals between ports not friendly to her, and the United States was one of the chief sufferers from the extraordinary assumptions of the two hostile powers.

To save our vessels from depredation President Jefferson recommended what is known as the Embargo, which prevented the departure of our vessels from our own ports, and thus of course suspended our commercial relations with the rest of the world. The Embargo was never a popular measure, and its effects were felt to be widely injurious. I do not propose to discuss the question, but merely to state that in 1808 Mr. Webster published a pamphlet upon the Embargo, and, as his biographer claims, this must be regarded as his first appearance in a public character. I must refer such of my readers as desire more fully to understand the condition of public affairs and the part that the young lawyer took therein to the first volume of Mr. Curtis's memoir.

It may be stated here, however, to explain the special interest which he felt in the matter, that Portsmouth, as a seaport, was largely affected by the suspension of American commerce, and its citizens felt an interest easily explained in what was so disastrous to their business prosperity.

On the Fourth of July, 1812, Mr. Webster delivered by invitation an oration before the "Washington Benevolent Society," of Portsmouth, in which he discussed in a vigorous way the policy of the government, which he did not approve. Sixteen days before Congress had declared war against England. To this war Mr. Webster was opposed. Whatever grievances the government may have suffered from England, he contended that there was "still more abundant cause of war against France." Moreover America was not prepared for war. The navy had been suffered to fall into neglect during Jefferson's administration, until it was utterly insufficient for the defense of our coasts and harbors.

On this point he says: " If the plan of Washington had been pursued, and our navy had been suffered to grow with the growth of our commerce and navigation, what a blow might at this moment be struck, and what protection yielded, surrounded, as our commerce now is, with all the dangers of sudden war! Even as it is, all our immediate hopes of glory or conquest, all expectation of events that shall gratify the pride or spirit of the nation, rest on the gallantry of that little remnant of a navy that has now gone forth, like lightning, at the beck of Government, to scour the seas.

"It will not be a bright page in our history which relates the total abandonment of all provision for naval defense by the successors of Washington. Not to speak of policy and expediency, it will do no credit to the national faith, stipulated and plighted as it was to that object in every way that could make the engagement solemn and obligatory. So long as our commerce remains unprotected, and our coasts and harbors undefended by naval and maritime means, the essential objects of the Union remain unanswered, and the just expectation of those who assented to it, unanswered.

"A part of our navy has been suffered to go to entire decay; another part has been passed, like an article of useless lumber, under the hammer of the auctioneer. As if the millennium had already commenced, our politicians have beaten their swords into plowshares. They have actually bargained away in the market essential means of national defense, and carried the product to the Treasury. Without loss by accident or by enemies the second commercial nation in the world is reduced to the limitation of being unable to assert the sovereignty of its own seas, or to protect its navigation in sight of its own shores. What war and the waves have sometimes done for others, we have done for ourselves. We have taken the destruction of our marine out of the power of fortune, and richly achieved it by our own counsels."

This address made a profound impression, voicing as it did the general public feeling in New Hampshire on the subjects of which it treated. It led to an assembly of the people of Rockingham County a few weeks later, called to prepare a memorial to the President protesting against the war. To this convention Mr. Webster was appointed a delegate, and it was he who was selected to draft what has been since known as the "Rockingham Memorial."

One of the most noteworthy passages in this memorial—noteworthy because it is an early expression of his devotion to the Union—I find quoted by Mr. Curtis, and I shall follow his lead in transferring it to my pages.

"We are, sir, from principle and habit attached to the Union of these States. But our attachment is to the substance, and not to the form. It is to the good which this Union is capable of producing, and not to the evil which is suffered unnaturally to grow out of it. If the time should ever arrive when this Union shall be holden together by nothing but the authority of law; when its incorporating, vital principles shall become extinct; when its principal exercises shall consist in acts of power and authority, not of protection and beneficence; when it shall lose the strong bond which it hath hitherto had in the public affections; and when, consequently, we shall be one, not in interest and mutual regard, but in name and form only—we, sir, shall look on that hour as the closing scene of our country's prosperity.

"We shrink from the separation of the States as an event fraught with incalculable evils, and it is among our strongest objections to the present course of measures that they have, in our opinion, a very dangerous and alarming bearing on such an event. If a separation of the States ever should take place, it will be on some occasion when one portion of the country undertakes to control, to regulate and to sacrifice the interest of another; when a small and heated majority in the Government, taking counsel of their passions, and not of their reason, contemptuously disregarding the interests and perhaps stopping the mouths of a large and respectable minority, shall by hasty, rash and ruinious measures, threaten to destroy essential rights, and lay waste the most important interests.

"It shall be our most fervent supplication to Heaven to avert both the event and the occasion; and the Government may be assured that the tie that binds us to the Union will never be broken by us."

Even my young readers will be struck by the judicial calmness, the utter absence of heated partisanship, which mark the extracts I have made, and they will recall the passage well known to every schoolboy—the grand closing passage of the reply to Hayne.

As regards style it will be seen that, though yet a young man, Mr. Webster had made a very marked advance on the Fourth of July address which he delivered while yet a college-student. He was but thirty years old when the memorial was drafted, and in dignified simplicity and elevation of tone it was worthy of his later days.

The young lawyer, whose time had hitherto been employed upon cases of trifling moment in a country town, had been ripening his powers, and expanding into the intellectual proportions of a statesman. It was evident at any rate that his neighbors thought so, for he was nominated as a Representative to the Thirteenth Congress, in due time elected, and, as has already been stated, he first took his seat at a special session called by the President on the 24th of May, 1813.

It was in this Congress that Daniel Webster made the acquaintance of two eminent men, with whose names his own is now most frequently associated—Henry Clay, of Kentucky, and John C. Calhoun, of South Carolina.

CHAPTER XXII.

MR. WEBSTER AS A MEMBER OF CONGRESS.

BEFORE I proceed to speak of Mr. Webster's Congressional career, I will make room for a professional anecdote, which carries with it an excellent lesson for my young readers.

I find it in Harvey's "Reminiscences," already alluded to.

"In the first years of his professional life a blacksmith called on him for advice respecting the title to a small estate bequeathed to him by his father. The terms of the will were peculiar, and the kind of estate transmitted was doubtful. An attempt had been made to annull the will. Mr. Webster examined the case, but was unable to give a definite opinion upon the matter for want of authorities. He looked through the law libraries of Mr. Mason and other legal gentlemen for authorities, but in vain. He ascertained what works he needed for consultation, and ordered them from Boston at an expense of fifty dollars. He spent the leisure hours of some weeks in going through them. He successfully argued the case when it came on for trial, and it was decided in his favor.

"The blacksmith was in ecstasies, for his little all had been at stake. He called for his attorney's bill. Mr. Webster, knowing his poverty, charged him only fifteen dollars, intending to suffer the loss of money paid out, and to lose the time expended in securing a verdict. Years passed away, and the case was forgotten, but not the treasured knowledge by which it was won. On one of his journeys to Washington Mr. Webster spent a few days in New York City. While he was there Aaron Burr waited on him for advice in a very important case pending in the State court. He told him the facts on which it was founded. Mr. Webster saw in a moment that it was an exact counterpart to the blacksmith's will case. On being asked if he could state the law applicable to it he at once replied that he could.

"He proceeded to quote decisions bearing upon the case, going back to the time of Charles II. As he went on with his array of principles and authorities, all cited with the precision and order of a table of contents, Mr. Burr arose in astonishment and asked with some warmth,

"'Mr. Webster, have you been consulted before in this case?'

"'Most certainly not,' he replied. 'I never heard of your case till this evening.'

"'Very well,' said Mr. Burr; 'proceed.'

"Mr. Webster concluded the rehearsal of his authorities, and received from Mr. Burr the warmest praise of his profound knowledge of the law, and a fee large enough to remunerate him for all the time and trouble spent on the blacksmith's case."

I have recorded this anecdote, partly to show the tenacity of Mr. Webster's memory, which, after a lapse of years, enabled him so exactly to repeat the authorities he had relied upon in an old case; partly, also, to show how thoroughly he was wont to prepare himself, even in cases where he could expect but a small fee. In this case, not only did he subsequently turn his knowledge to profitable account, but he lost nothing by the kindness of heart which prompted him to place his best powers at the service of an humble client. My young readers will find that knowledge never comes amiss, but, in the course of a long and sometimes of a short life, we are generally able to employ it for our advantage.

I come back to Daniel Webster's entrance upon Congressional duties.

He had reached the age of thirty-one, while Henry Clay, who occupied the Speaker's chair, was five years older. Mr. Clay came forward much earlier in public life than his great rival. Though but thirty-six, he had twice been a member of the United States Senate, being in each case elected to serve the balance of an unexpired term. He had been a member of the Legislature of Kentucky, and Speaker of that body, and now he was serving, not for the first time, as Speaker of the U. S. House of Representatives. John C. Calhoun was the leading member of the House, and he as well as Mr. Clay favored the policy of the administration, both being supporters of the war. Other distinguished members there were, among them John McLean, of Ohio; Charles J. Ingersoll, of Pennsylvania; William Gaston, of North Carolina, and Felix Grundy, of Tennessee.

Though Mr. Webster was a new member he was placed upon the Committee on Foreign Relations, at that time of course the most important position which could have been assigned him. This may be inferred from the names of his fellow members. He found himself associated with Calhoun, Grundy, Jackson, Fish and Ingersoll. He was, as I have stated, not in favor of the war, but since it had been inaugurated he took the ground that it should be vigorously prosecuted. He did not long remain silent, but took his stand both in the committee and in the House as one who thought the war inexpedient.

It does not fall within the scope of this volume to detail the steps which the young member took in order to impress his views upon his fellow members; but, as a specimen of his oratory at that time, and because it will explain them sufficiently, I quote from a speech made by him in the regular session during the year 1814:

"The humble aid which it would be in my power to render to measures of Government shall be given cheerfully, if Government will pursue measures which I can conscientiously support. Badly as I think of the original grounds of the war, as well as of the manner in which it has hitherto been conducted, if even now, failing in an honest and sincere attempt to procure just and honorable peace, it will return to measures of defence and protection such as reason and common sense and the public opinion all call for, my vote shall not be withholden from the means. Give up your futile object of invasion. Extinguish the fires that blaze on your inland frontier. Establish perfect safety and defense there by adequate force. Let every man that sleeps on your soil sleep in security. Stop the blood that flows from the veins of unarmed yeomanry and women and children. Give to the living time to bury and lament their dead in the quietness of private sorrow.

"Having performed this work of beneficence and mercy on your inland border, turn and look with the eye of justice and compassion on your vast population along the coast. Unclinch the iron grasp of your Embargo. Take measures for that end before another sun sets upon you. With all the war of the enemy on your commerce, if you would cease to war on it yourselves you would still have some commerce. Apply that revenue to the augmentation of your navy. That navy will in turn protect your commerce. Let it no longer be said that not one ship of force, built by your hands, yet floats upon the ocean.

"Turn the current of your efforts into the channel which national sentiment has already worn broad and deep to receive it. A naval force, competent to defend your coast against considerable armaments, to convoy your trade, and perhaps raise the blockade of your rivers, is not a chimera. It may be realized. If, then, the war must be continued, go to the ocean. If you are seriously contending for maritime rights, go to the theater where alone those rights can be defended. Thither every indication of your fortune points you. There the united wishes and exertions of the nation will go with you. Even our party divisions, acrimonious as they are, cease at the water's edge. They are lost in attachment to national character on the element where that character is made respectable. In protecting naval interests by naval means, you will arm yourselves with the whole power of national sentiment, and may command the whole abundance of the national resources. In time you may enable yourselves to redress injuries in the place where they may be offered, and, if need be, to accompany your own flag throughout the world with the protection of your own cannon."

My young reader, without knowing much about the matter at issue, will nevertheless be struck with the statesmanlike character of these utterances. It is not often that a new member of Congress is able to discuss public matters with such fullness of knowledge, and in a tone of such dignity and elevation of sentiment. His fellow legislators were not long in learning that the new member from New Hampshire was no raw novice, but a publicist of remarkable ability, knowledge, and a trained orator. In a discussion which sprang up between Mr. Webster and Mr. Calhoun, the conceded leader of the House, the honors were at least divided, if Mr. Webster did not win the larger portion.

While the young man was thus coming into

national prominence his residence in Washington helped him in a professional way. He began to practice in the Supreme Court of the United States, being employed in several prize cases. Judge Marshall was at that time chief justice, and of him the young lawyer formed an exalted opinion. "I have never seen a man," he writes, "of whose intellect I had a higher opinion."

On the 18th of April, 1814, the session of Congress terminated, and Mr. Webster undertook the long and toilsome journey from Washington to his New Hampshire home. It was not the same home which he left when he was called a year earlier to attend the special session. His house and library were destroyed by fire, and though the loss was but six thousand dollars, it was a severe set-back to a lawyer whose professional income had never exceeded two thousand dollars. He bore the loss, however, with equanimity, since it involved only a loss of money. His talent and education remained, and these were to earn him hundreds of thousands of dollars in the years to come.

CHAPTER XXIII.

JOHN RANDOLPH AND WILLIAM PINKNEY.

MR. WEBSTER served four years in Congress as a Representative from his native State. He had reached the age of thirty-one when he entered the public service, and therefore, though not the youngest, was among the youngest members of that important body. As we have seen, though without previous legislative experience, he advanced at once to a leading place and took prominent part in all the discussions of important questions, his opinions always carrying weight. He was opposed to the administration and its war policy, but he opposed it in no factious spirit.

He distinguished himself particularly by his speeches on finance. When a bill was proposed to establish a national bank, with a capital of fifty millions of dollars, of which only four millions was to be specie, and the balance to consist of Government stocks, then very much depreciated, Mr. Webster rode forty miles on horseback from

Baltimore to Washington, in order to defeat what he regarded as a scheme to create an irredeemable paper currency, fraught with widespread mischief to the country. The vigorous speech which he made defeated the bill. It is interesting to record that Mr. Calhoun, when the vote was announced, walked across the floor of the House to where Mr. Webster stood, and holding out both hands to him, told him that he should rely upon his help to prepare a new bill of a proper character. When this assurance was given Mr. Calhoun's feelings were so stirred that he burst into tears, so deeply did he feel the importance of some aid for the Government, which he felt with Mr. Webster's co-operation might be secured.

It may be stated here that these great men cherished for each other mutual respect and friendship, widely as they differed on some points. The Senator from South Carolina showed this in a notable manner when he arose from his deathbed (his death followed in a few days), and sat in his place to listen to his great friend's seventh of March speech, in 1850, looking a wan and spectral auditor from the next world.

The battle for sound money which Mr. Webster fought then has been renewed in later years, as some of my young readers may be aware. In his speeches he showed a thorough mastery of the subject which he discussed. He showed the evils of a debased coin, a depreciated paper currency, and a depressed and falling public credit, and it is largely due to his efforts that the country emerged from its chaotic financial condition with as little injury as it did.

I have spoken of Mr. Webster's relations then and later to Mr. Calhoun. Among the members of the House representing Virginia was the famous John Randolph, of Roanoke, with whom it was difficult for any one to keep on good terms. He saw fit to take offense at something said by Mr. Webster, and sent him a challenge. Webster was never charged by any man with physical cowardice, but he thoroughly despised the practice of dueling. He was not to be coerced into fighting by any fear that cowardice would be imputed to him. This may seem to us a very trivial matter, but seventy years ago and even much later, it required considerable moral courage to refuse a challenge. I place on record, as likely to interest my readers, the letter in which Mr. Webster declined to give satisfaction in the manner demanded.

"SIR: For having declined to comply with your demand yesterday in the House for an explanation of words of a general nature used in debate, you now 'demand of me that satisfaction which your insulted feelings require,' and refer me to your friend, Mr. ——, I presume, as he is the bearer of your note, for such arrangements as are usual.

"This demand for explanation you, in my judgment, as a matter of right were not entitled to make on me, nor were the temper and style of your own reply to my objection to the sugar tax of a character to induce me to accord it as a matter of courtesy.

"Neither can I, under the circumstances of the case, recognize in you a right to call me to the field to answer what you may please to consider an insult to your feelings.

"It is unnecessary for me to state other and obvious considerations growing out of this case. It is enough that I do not feel myself bound at all times and under any circumstances to accept from any man who shall choose to risk his own life an invitation of this sort, although I shall be always prepared to repel in a suitable manner the aggression of any man who may presume upon such a refusal.

"Your obedient servant,
"DANIEL WEBSTER."

Mr. Randolph did not press the matter nor did he presume upon the refusal, but the matter was adjusted amicably. Nearly forty years later a similar reply to a challenge was sent by a later Senator from Massachusetts, Henry Wilson, and in both cases the resolute character of the men was so well known that no one dared to taunt the writer with cowardice.

While upon the subject of physical courage I am tempted to transcribe from Mr. Harvey's interesting volume an anecdote in which the famous lawyer, William Pinkney, is prominently mentioned. In answer to the question whether he ever carried pistols, Mr. Webster answered:

"No, I never did. I always trusted to my strong arm, and I do not believe in pistols. There were some Southern men whose blood was hot and who got very much excited in debate, and I used myself to get excited, but I never resorted to any such extremity as the use of pistols.

"The nearest I ever came to a downright row was with Mr. William Pinkney. Mr. Pinkney was the acknowledged head and leader of the American bar. He was the great practitioner at Washington when I was admitted to practice in the courts there. I found Mr. Pinkney by universal concession the very head of the bar—a lawyer of extraordinary accomplishments and withal a very wonderful man. But with all that there was something about him that was very small. He did things that one would hardly think it possible that a gentleman of his breeding and culture and great weight as a lawyer could do.

"He was a very vain man. One saw it in every motion he made. When he came into court he was dressed in the very extreme of fashion—almost like a dandy. He would wear into the court-room his white gloves that had been put on fresh that morning and that he never put on again. He usually rode from his house to the Capitol on horseback, and his overalls were taken off and given to his servant who attended him. Pinkney showed in his whole appearance that he considered himself the great man of that arena, and that he expected deference to be paid to him as the acknowledged leader of the bar. He had a great many satellites—men of course much less eminent than himself at the bar—who flattered him, and employed him to take their briefs and argue their cases, they doing the work and he receiving the greatest share of the pay. That was the position that Mr. Pinkney occupied when I entered the bar at Washington.

"I was a lawyer who had my living to get, and I felt that although I should not argue my cases as well as he could, still, if my clients employed me they should have the best ability I had to give them, and I should do the work myself. I did not propose to practice law in the Supreme Court by proxy. I think that in some pretty important cases I had Mr. Pinkney rather expected that I should fall into the current of his admirers and share my fees with him. This I utterly refused to do.

"In some important case (I have forgotten what the case was) Mr. Pinkney was employed to argue it against me. I was going to argue it for my client myself. I had felt that on several occasions his manner was, to say the least, very annoying and aggravating. My intercourse with him, so far as I had any, was always marked with great courtesy and deference. I regarded him as the leader of the American bar; he had that reputation and justly. He was a very great lawyer. On the occasion to which I refer, in some colloquial discussion upon various minor points of the case he treated me with contempt. He poohpoohed, as much as to say it was not worth while to argue a point that I did not know anything about, that I was no lawyer. I think he spoke of 'the gentleman from New Hampshire.' At any rate, it was a thing that everybody in the court-house, including the judges, could not fail to observe. Chief Justice Marshall himself was pained by it. It was very hard for me to restrain my temper and keep cool, but I did so, knowing in what presence I stood. I think he construed my apparent humility into a want of what he would call spirit in resisting, and as a sort of acquiescence in his rule.

"However the incident passed, the case was not finished when the hour for adjournment came, and the court adjourned until the next morning.

"Mr. Pinkney took his whip and gloves, threw his cloak over his arm, and began to saunter away.

"I went up to him and said very calmly, 'Can I see you alone in one of the lobbies?'

"He replied, 'Certainly.' I suppose he thought I was going to beg his pardon and ask his assistance. We passed one of the anterooms of the Capitol. I looked into one of the grand jury rooms, rather remote from the main court-room. There was no one in it, and we entered. As we did so I looked at the door, and found that there was a key in the lock; and, unobserved by him, I turned the key and put it in my pocket. Mr. Pinkney seemed to be waiting in some astonishment.

"I advanced towards him and said: 'Mr. Pinkney, you grossly insulted me in the court-room, and not for the first time either. In deference to your position, and to the respect in which I hold the court, I did not answer you as I was tempted to do on the spot.'

"He began to parley.

"I continued. 'You know you did; don't add another sin to that; don't deny it; you know you did it, and you know it was premeditated. It was deliberate; it was purposely done; and if you deny it, you state an untruth. Now,' I went on, 'I am here to say to you, once for all, that you must ask my pardon, and go into court to-morrow morning and repeat the apology, or else either you or I will go out of this room in a different condition from that in which we entered it.'

"I was never more in earnest. He looked at me, and saw that my eyes were pretty dark and firm. He began to say something. I interrupted him.

"'No explanation,' said I; 'admit the fact, and take it back. I do not want another word from you except that. I will hear no explanation; nothing but that you admit it and recall it.'

"He trembled like an aspen leaf. He again attempted to explain.

"Said I, 'There is no other course. I have the key in my pocket, and you must apologize, or take what I give you.'

"At that he humbled down, and said to me: 'You are right, I am sorry; I did intend to bluff you; I regret it, and ask your pardon.'

"'Enough,' I promptly replied. 'Now, one promise before I open the door; and that is, that you will to-morrow state to the court that you have said things which wounded my feelings, and that you regret it.'

"Pinkney replied, 'I will do so.'

"Then I unlocked the door, and passed out.

"The next morning, when the court met, Mr. Pinkney at once rose, and stated to the court that a very unpleasant affair had occurred the morning before, as might have been observed by their honors; that his friend, Mr. Webster, had felt grieved at some things which had dropped from his lips; that his zeal for his client might have led him to say some things which he should not have said, and that he was sorry for having thus spoken.'

"From that day," adds Mr. Webster, "there was no man who treated me with so much respect and deference as Mr. William Pinkney."

I have recorded this anecdote that my young readers may understand clearly that the young lawyer was manly and self-respecting, and declined the method of satisfaction then in vogue from high and honorable motives.

CHAPTER XXIV.

MR. WEBSTER IN BOSTON.

BEFORE his second Congressional term had expired, Mr. Webster carried out a plan which was first suggested by the destruction of his house and library. His talents demanded a wider arena. Moreover, his growing family necessitated a style of living for which his professional income was insufficient. Happily as his life had flowed on in the chief town in his native State, he felt that he must seek a new residence. For a time he hesitated between Albany and Boston but happily for the latter he decided in its favor, and in August, 1816, he removed thither with his family, fixing his home in a house on Mt. Vernon Street, but a few rods from the State House.

It mattered not where Daniel Webster might choose to locate himself, he was sure to take at once a leading position both as a lawyer and a man. He was now thirty-four years old. He had outlived his early delicacy, and began to assume that dignity and majesty of mein which made him everywhere a marked man. Appearances are oftentimes deceptive, but in his case it was not so. That outward majesty which has been quaintly described in the statement that "when Daniel Webster walked the streets of Boston he made the buildings look small," was but the sign and manifestation of a corresponding intellectual greatness. By his removal New Hampshire lost her greatest son, and Boston gained its foremost citizen.

His expectations of a largely increased professional income were fully realized. In Portsmouth his fees had never exceeded two thousand dollars per year. The third year after his removal his fee-book foots up over fifteen thousand dollars as the receipts of a single year, and this record is probably incomplete. His biographer, Mr. Curtis, says: "I am satisfied that his income, from 1818 until he again entered Congress in 1823, could not have been on an average less than $20,000 a year, though the customary fees of such counsel at that time were about one half of what they are now." Now, for the first time, he was able to pay in full his father's debts, which he had voluntarily assumed declining to have his small estate thrown into bankruptcy.

I shall have occasion, hereafter, to point out with regret the fact that his expenses increased even more rapidly than his income, and that he voluntarily incurred debts and pecuniary obligations which all his life long harassed him, and held him in an entirely unnecessary thraldom. On the subject of national finance Mr. Webster, as we have seen, held the soundest views; but in the management of his own finances, for the larger portion of his active life he displayed an incapacity to control his expenditures and confine them within his income which caused his best friends to grieve. In this respect, at any rate, I cannot present the hero whom we so deservedly admire as a mode.

The large increase in Mr. Webster's income is sufficient to prove that he was employed in the most important cases. But fifteen years had elapsed since, as a raw graduate of a country college, he humbly sought an opportunity to study in the office of a well-known Boston lawyer. Now he took his place at the bar, and rapidly gained a much higher position than the man who had kindly extended to him a welcome. It is to the credit of Mr. Gore's ability to read character and judge of ability that he foresaw and predicted all this when through his influence his student was led to decline the clerkship of a New Hampshire court, which then would have filled the measure of his ambition.

And how was all this gained? I can assure my young readers that no great lawyer, no great writer, no great member of any profession, lounges into greatness. Daniel Webster worked, and worked hard. He rose early, not only because it gave him an opportunity of doing considerable while he was fresh and elastic, but because he had a country boy's love of nature. Whether in city or country, the early morning hours were dear to him. As Mr. Lee says, "He did a large amount of work before others were awake in the house, and in the evening he was ready for that sweet sleep which 'God gives to his beloved.'"

During the period which elapsed between his arrival in Boston and his return to Congress as a Representative of his adopted city his life was crowded, and he appeared in many notable cases. But there was one which merits special mention, because he was enabled to do a great service to the college where he had been educated, and prove himself in a signal manner a grateful and loyal son.

Of the celebrated Dartmouth College case I do not consider it necessary for my present purpose to speak in detail. It is sufficient to say that it was menaced with a serious peril. The chartered rights of the college were threatened by legislative interference; nay, more, an act was passed, and pronounced valid by the courts of New Hampshire, which imperilled the usefulness and prosperity of the institution. The matter was carried before the Supreme Court of the United States, and Mr. Webster's services were secured. The argument which he made on that occasion established his reputation as a great lawyer. The closing portion was listened to with absorbing interest. It was marked by deep feeling on the part of the speaker. It is as follows:

"This, sir, is my case. It is the case not merely of that humble institution, it is the case of every college in our land; it is more, it is the case of every eleemosynary institution throughout our country—of all those great charities founded by the piety of our ancestors, to alleviate human misery, and scatter blessings along the pathway of life. It is more! It is, in some sense, the case of every man among us who has property of which he may stripped, for the question is simply this: 'Shall our State Legislatures be allowed to take that which is not their own, to turn it from its original use, and apply it to such ends or purposes as they in their discretion shall see fit?'

'Sir, you may destroy this little institution

it is weak; it is in your hands. I know it is one of the lesser lights in the literary horizon of our country. You may put it out. But if you do so, you must carry through your work! You must extinguish, one after another, all those greater lights of science which, for more than a century, have thrown their light over our land!

"It is, sir, as I have said, a small college, and yet there are those who love it—"

Here the orator was overcome by emotion. His lips quivered, and his eyes filled with tears. The effect was extraordinary. All who heard him, from Chief Justice Marshall to the humblest attendant, were borne away on the tide of emotion as he gave expression in a few broken words to the tenderness which he felt for his Alma Mater.

When he recovered his composure, he continued in deep, thrilling tones, "Sir, I know not how others may feel, but for myself, when I see my Alma Mater surrounded, like Cæsar in the Senate-house, by those who are reiterating stab after stab, I would not, for this right hand, have her turn to me, and say, 'Et tu quoque mi fili! And thou too, my son!'"

This speech, which was masterly in point of logic as well as a powerful appeal to the feelings, was successful, and the opponents of the college were disastrously defeated.

CHAPTER XXV.

THE ORATION AT PLYMOUTH.

THE three-fold character in which Daniel Webster achieved greatness was as lawyer, orator and statesman. In this respect he must be placed at the head of the immortal three whose names are usually conjoined. Mr. Calhoun did not pretend to be a lawyer, and Mr. Clay, though he practiced law, possessed but a small share of legal erudition, and when he gained cases, was indebted to his eloquence rather than to his mastery of the legal points involved. Both, however, may claim to be orators and statesmen, but even in these respects it is probable that the highest place would be accorded to their great compeer.

Up to the age of thirty-eight Mr. Webster had not vindicated his claim to the title of a great orator. In Congress and in his profession he had shown himself a powerful, eloquent and convincing speaker, but it was not until he delivered at Plymouth his celebrated discourse on the two hundredth anniversary of the settlement that he established his fame as a great anniversary orator.

Probably no better selection of an orator could have been made. The circumstances of his own early career, born and brought up as he was on the sterile soil of one of the original States of New England, trained like the first settlers in the rugged school of poverty and simplicity, wresting a bare subsistence from unwilling nature, he could enter into the feelings of those hardy men who brought the seeds of civilization and civil liberty from the shores of the Old World to find a lodgment for them in the soil of the New. He could appreciate and admire the spirit which actuated them, and no one was more likely to set a proper value on the results they achieved.

So, by a happy conjuncture, the orator fitted the occasion, and the occasion was of a character to draw forth the best powers of the orator. It gave him an opportunity to pay a fitting tribute to the virtues of the stern but conscientious and deeply religious men, who had their faults indeed, but who in spite of them will always receive not only from their descendants but from the world a high measure of respect. Of the oration, the manner in which it was delivered, and its effect upon his audience, we have this account by an eye and ear witness, Mr. Ticknor:

"In the morning I went with Mr. Webster to

the church where he was to deliver the oration. It was the old First Church—Dr. Kendall's. He did not find the pulpit convenient for his purpose, and after making two or three experiments, determined to speak from the deacon's seat under it. An extemporaneous table, covered with a green baize cloth, was arranged for the occasion, and when the procession entered the church everything looked very appropriate, though when the arrangement was first suggested it sounded rather odd.

"The building was crowded; indeed, the streets had seemed so all the morning, for the weather was fine, and the whole population was astir as for a holiday. The oration was an hour and fifty minutes long, but the whole of what was printed a year afterwards (for a year before it made its appearance) was not delivered. His manner was very fine—quite various in the different parts. The passage about the slave trade was delivered with a power of indignation such as I never witnessed on any other occasion. That at the end when, spreading his arms as if to embrace them, he welcomed future generations to the great inheritance which we have enjoyed, was spoken with the most attractive sweetness, and that peculiar smile which in him was always so charming.

"The effect of the whole was very great. As soon as he got home to our lodgings all the principal people then in Plymouth crowded about him. He was full of animation and radiant with happiness. But there was something about him very grand and imposing at the same time. In a letter which I wrote the same day I said that 'he seemed as if he were like the mount that might not be touched, and that burned with fire.' I have the same recollection of him still. I never saw him at any time when he seemed to me to be more conscious of his own powers, or to have a more true and natural enjoyment from their possession."

The occasion will always be memorable, for on that day it was revealed to the world that America possessed an orator fit to be ranked with the greatest orators of ancient or modern times. A year afterwards John Adams, in a letter to Mr. Webster, said of it: "It is the effort of a great mind, richly stored with every species of information. If there be an American who can read it without tears I am not that American. It enters more perfectly into the genuine spirit of New England than any production I ever read. The observations on the Greeks and Romans; on colonization in general; on the West India Islands; on the past, present and future of America, and on the slave trade are sagacious, profound and affecting in a high degree. Mr. Burke is no longer entitled to the praise, the most consummate orator of modern times. This oration will be read five hundred years hence with as much rapture as it was heard. It ought to be read at the end of every century, and indeed at the end of every year, forever and ever."

This testimony is the more interesting because the writer less then five years later was himself, with his great contemporary, Mr. Jefferson, to be the subject of an address which will always be reckoned as one of Webster's masterpieces.

And now, since many of my young readers will never read the Plymouth oration, I surrender the rest of this chapter to two extracts which may give them an idea of its high merits.

"There are enterprises, military as well as civil, which sometimes check the current of events, give a new turn to human affairs, and transmit their consequences through ages. We see their importance in their results, and call them great because great things follow. There have been battles which have fixed the fate of nations. These come down to us in history with a solid and permanent interest, not created by a display of glittering armor, the rush of adverse battalions, the sinking and rising of pennons, the flight, the pursuit and the victory; but by their effect in advancing or retarding human knowledge, in overthrowing or establishing despotism, in extending or destroying human happiness.

"When the traveler pauses on the plain of Marathon, what are the emotions which most strongly agitate his breast? What is that glorious recollection which thrills through his frame and suffuses his eyes? Not, I imagine, that Grecian skill and Grecian valor were here most signally displayed, but that Greece herself was here displayed. It is because to this spot, and to the event which has rendered it immortal, he refers all the succeeding glories of the republic. It is because, if that day had gone otherwise, Greece had perished. It is because he perceives that her philosophers and orators, her poets and painters, her sculptors and architects, her government and free institutions, point backward to Marathon, and that their future existence seems to have been suspended on the contingency whether the Persian or the Grecian banner should wave victorious in the beams of that day's setting sun. And, as his imagination kindles at the retrospect, he is transported back to the interesting moment, he counts the fearful odds of the contending hosts, his interest for the result overwhelms him, he trembles as if it were still uncertain, and grows to doubt whether he may consider Socrates and Plato, Demosthenes, Sophocles and Phidias, as secure yet to himself and the world.

"'If God prosper us,' might have been the appropriate language of our fathers when they landed upon this Rock. If God prosper us, we shall begin a work which shall last for ages; we shall plant here a new society in the principles of the fullest liberty and the purest religion; we shall fill this region of the great continent, which stretches almost from pole to pole, with civilization and Christianity; the temples of the true God shall rise, where now ascends the smoke of idolatrous sacrifice; fields and gardens, the flowers of summer and the waving and golden harvest of autumn shall extend over a thousand hills and stretch along a thousand valleys never yet, since the creation, reclaimed to the use of civilized man.

"We shall whiten this coast with the canvas of a prosperous commerce; we shall stud the long and winding shore with a hundred cities. That which we sow in weakness shall be raised in strength. From our sincere but houseless worship there shall spring splendid temples to record God's goodness, and from the simplicity of our social unions there shall arise wise and politic constitutions of government, full of the liberty which we ourselves bring and breathe; from our zeal for learning institutions shall spring which shall scatter the light of knowledge throughout the land, and, in time, paying back where they have borrowed, shall contribute their part to the great aggregate of human knowledge; and our descendants through all generations shall look back to this spot, and to this hour, with unabated affection and regard."

I close with the solemn and impressive peroration in which the orator addresses those who are to come after him.

"Advance then, ye future generations! We would hail you as you rise in your long succession to fill the places which we now fill, and to taste the blessings of existence where we are passing, and soon shall have passed, our own human duration. We bid you welcome to this pleasant land of the fathers. We bid you welcome to the healthful skies and the verdant fields of New England. We greet your accession to the great inheritance which we have enjoyed. We welcome you to the blessings of good government and religious liberty. We welcome you to the treasures of science and the delights of learning. We welcome you to the transcendent sweets of domestic life, to the happiness of kindred and parents and children. We welcome you to the immeasurable blessings of rational existence, the immortal hope of Christianity, and the light of everlasting truth!"

CHAPTER XXVI.

THE BUNKER HILL ORATION.

THE oration at Plymouth first revealed the power of Mr. Webster. There are some men who exhaust themselves in one speech, one poem, or one story, and never attain again the high level which they have once reached.

It was not so with Daniel Webster. He had a fund of reserved power which great occasions never drew upon in vain. It might be that in an ordinary case in court, where his feelings were not aroused, and no fitting demand made upon his great abilities, he would disappoint the expectations of those who supposed that he must always be eloquent. I heard a gentleman say once, "Oh, I heard Mr. Webster speak once, and his speech was commonplace enough."

"On what occasion?"

"In court."

"What was the case?"

"Oh, I don't remember — some mercantile case."

It would certainly be unreasonable to expect any man to invest dry commercial details with eloquence. Certainly a lawyer always ambitious in his rhetoric would hardly commend himself to a sound, sensible client.

But Mr. Webster always rose to the level of a great occasion. His occasional speeches were always carefully prepared and finished, and there is not one of them but will live. I now have to call special attention to the address delivered at the laying of the corner-stone of Bunker Hill Monument, at Charlestown, June 17, 1825. It was an occasion from which he could not help drawing inspiration. His father, now dead, whom he had loved and revered as few sons love and revere their parents, had been a participant, not indeed in the battle which the granite shaft was to commemorate, but in the struggle which the colonists waged for liberty. It may well be imagined that Mr. Webster gazed with no common emotion at the veterans who were present to hear their patriotism celebrated. Though the passages addressed to them—in part at least—are familiar to many of my readers, I will nevertheless quote them here. Apart from their subject they will never be forgotten by Americans.

"Venerable men! you have come down to us from a former generation. Heaven has boun-

teously lengthened out your lives that you might
behold this joyous day. You are now where you
stood fifty years ago, this very hour, with your
brothers and your neighbors, shoulder to shoulder in the strife of your country. Behold how
altered! The same heavens are indeed over your
heads; the same ocean rolls at your feet; but all
else how changed! You hear now no roar of
hostile cannon, you see now no mixed volumes of
smoke and flame rising from burning Charlestown. The ground strewed with the dead and
the dying; the impetuous charge; the steady
and successful repulse; the loud call to repeated
assault; the summoning of all that is manly to
repeated resistance; a thousand bosoms freely and
fearlessly bared in an instant to whatever of terror
there may be in war and death—all these you have
witnessed, but you witness them no more.

"All is peace. The heights of yonder metro-
polis, its towers and roofs, which you then saw
filled with wives and children and countrymen in
distress and terror, and looking with unutterable
emotions for the issue of the combat, have pre-
sented you to-day with the sight of its whole happy
population come out to welcome and greet you
with an universal jubilee. Yonder proud ships, by
a felicity of position appropriately lying at the foot
of this mound, and seeming fondly to cling around

it, are not means of annoyance to you, but your country's own means of distinction and defense. All is peace, and God has granted you this sight of your country's happiness ere you slumber forever in the grave; he has allowed you to behold and to partake the reward of your patriotic toils; and he has allowed us, your sons and countrymen, to meet you here, and in the name of the present generation, in the name of your country, in the name of liberty, to thank you!

"But, alas! you are not all here! Time and the sword have thinned your ranks. Prescott, Putnam, Stark, Brooks, Read, Pomeroy, Bridge! our eyes seek for you in vain amid this broken band. You are gathered to your fathers, and live only to your country in her grateful remembrance and your own bright example. But let us not too much grieve that you have met the common fate of men. You lived at least long enough to know that your work had been nobly and successfully accomplished. You lived to see your country's independence established, and to sheathe your swords from war. On the light of liberty you saw arise the light of peace, like

'another morn,
Risen on mid-noon;'

and the sky on which you closed your eyes was cloudless."

After a tribute to General Warren 'the first great martyr in this great cause,' Mr. Webster proceeds:

"Veterans, you are the remnants of many a well-fought field. You bring with you marks of honor from Trenton and Monmouth, from Yorktown, Camden, Bennington and Saratoga. Veterans of half a century, when in your youthful days you put everything at hazard in your country's cause, good as that cause was, and sanguine as youth is, still your fondest hopes did not stretch onward to an hour like this. At a period to which you could not reasonably have expected to arrive, at a moment of national prosperity such as you could never have foreseen, you are now met here to enjoy the fellowship of old soldiers, and to receive the overflowings of an universal gratitude.

"But your agitated countenances and your heaving breasts inform me that even this is not an unmixed joy. I perceive that a tumult of contending feelings rushes upon you. The images of the dead, as well as the persons of the living, throng to your embraces. The scene overwhelms you, and I turn from it. May the Father of all mercies smile upon your declining years and bless them! And when you shall here have exchanged your embraces, when you shall once more have pressed the hands which have been so often extended to give succor in adversity, or grasped in the exultation of victory, then look abroad into this lovely land which your young valor defended, and mark the happiness with which it is filled; yea, look abroad into the whole earth, and see what a name you have contributed to give your country, and what a praise you have added to freedom, and then rejoice in the sympathy and gratitude which beam upon your last days from the improved condition of mankind!"

Not only were there war-scarred veterans present to listen entranced to the glowing periods of the inspired orator, but there was an eminent friend of America, a son of France, General Lafayette, who sat in a conspicuous seat and attracted the notice of all. To him the orator addressed himself in a manner no less impressive.

"Fortunate, fortunate man! with what measure of devotion will you not thank God for the circumstances of your extraordinary life! You are connected with both hemispheres, and with two generations. Heaven saw fit to ordain that the electric spark of liberty should be conducted, through you, from the New World to the Old; and we, who are now here to perform this duty of patriotism, have all of us long ago received it in charge from our fathers to cherish your name and your virtues. You will account it an instance of your good fortune, sir, that you crossed the seas to visit us at a time which enables you to be present at this solemnity. You now behold the field, the renown of which reached you in the heart of France, and caused a thrill in your ardent bosom; you see the lines of the little redoubt thrown up by the incredible diligence of Prescott, defended to the last extremity by his lion-hearted valor, and within which the corner-stone of our monument has now taken its position. You see where Warren fell, and where Parker, Gardner, McCleary, Moore and other early patriots fell with him. Those who survived that day, and whose lives have been prolonged to the present hour, are now around you. Some of them you have known in the trying scenes of the war. Behold! They now stretch forth their feeble arms to embrace you. Behold! They raise their trembling voices to invoke the blessing of God on you and yours forever."

I should like to increase my quotations, but space will not permit. I have quoted enough to give my young readers an idea of this masterly address. When next they visit the hill where the monument stands complete, let them try to picture to themselves how it looked on that occasion when, from the platform where he stood

Mr. Webster, with his clarion voice, facing the thousands who were seated before him on the rising hillside, and the other thousands who stood at the summit, spoke these eloquent words. Let them imagine the veteran soldiers, and the white-haired and venerable Lafayette, and they can better understand the effect which this address made on the eager and entranced listeners. They will not wonder at the tears which gathered in the eyes of the old soldiers as they bowed their heads to conceal their emotions. Surely there was no other man in America who could so admirably have improved the occasion.

CHAPTER XXVII.

ADAMS AND JEFFERSON.

July 4, 1826, was a memorable day. It was the fiftieth anniversary of American Independence, and for that reason, if no other, it was likely to be a day of note. But, by a singular coincidence, two eminent Americans, fathers of the republic, both of whom had filled the Presidency, yielded up their lives.

When John Adams was dying at Quincy, in Massachusetts, he spoke of his great countryman, Thomas Jefferson, who he naturally supposed was to survive him. But the same day, and that the natal day of the republic, brought the illustrious career of each to a close. Not untimely, for John Adams had passed the age of ninety, and Jefferson was but a few years younger.

Those were not the days of telegraphs nor of railroads, and the news had to be conveyed by stage-coaches, so that it was perhaps a month before the country through its large extent knew of the double loss which it had sustained. It was certainly by a most remarkable coincidence that these two great leaders, representing the two political parties which divided the country, but one in their devotion to the common welfare, passed from earthly scenes on the same anniversary. It was no wonder that they were the subjects of public addresses and sermons throughout the United States.

Of all those addresses but one is remembered to-day. It was the oration delivered by Daniel Webster on the 2d of August, 1826. This too was an anniversary, the anniversary of the day when the Declaration of Independence had been engrossed by the Revolutionary Congress.

As the circumstances attending the delivery of this oration will be new to my young readers, I quote from Mr. Ticknor's description, as I find it in Mr. Curtis's Life of Mr. Webster. After detailing an interview, in which Mr. Webster read him in advance some portions of the oration, he proceeds:

"The next day, the 2d of August, the weather was fine, and the concourse to hear him immense. It was the first time that Faneuil Hall had been draped in mourning. The scene was very solemn, though the light of day was not excluded. Settees had been placed over the whole area of the hall; the large platform was occupied by many of the most distinguished men in New England, and, as it was intended that everything should be conducted with as much quietness as possible, the doors were closed when the procession had entered, and every part of the hall and galleries was filled. This was a mistake in the arrangements; the crowd on the outside, thinking that some space must still be left within, became very uneasy, and finally grew so tumultuous and noisy that the solemnities were interrupted. The police in vain attempted to restore order. It seemed as if confusion would prevail. Mr. Webster perceived that there was but one thing to be done. He advanced to the front of the stage, and said in a voice easily heard above the noise of tumult without and of alarm within, '*Let those doors be opened.*'

"The power and authority of his manner were irresistible; the doors were opened, though with difficulty, from the pressure of the crowd on the outside; but after the first rush everything was quiet, and the order during the rest of the performance was perfect.

"Mr. Webster spoke in an orator's gown and wore small-clothes. He was in the perfection of his manly beauty and strength, his form filled out to its finest proportions, and his bearing, as he stood before the vast multitude, that of absolute dignity and power. His manuscript lay on a small table near him, but I think he did not once refer to it. His manner of speaking was deliberate and commanding. When he came to the passage on eloquence, and to the words, 'It is action, noble, sublime, godlike action,' he stamped his foot repeatedly on the stage, his form seemed to dilate, and he stood, as that whole audience saw and felt, the personification of what he so perfectly described. I never saw him when his manner was so grand and appropriate.

"The two speeches attributed to Mr. Adams and his opponent attracted great attention from the first. Soon they were put into school-books, as specimens of English and of eloquence. In time men began to believe they were genuine speeches, made by genuine men who were in the Congress of '76; and at last Mr. Webster received letters asking whether such was the fact or not. In January, 1846, he sent me from Washington a letter he had just received, dated at Auburn, begging him to solve the doubt. With it he sent me his answer, which is published in his works, saying: 'The accompanying letter and copy of answer respect a question which has been often asked me. I place them in your hands, to serve if similar inquiries should be made of you.' Two months after, in March of the same year, he sent me a letter from Bangor, in Maine, asking the same question, beginning the note which accompanied it with these words: 'Here comes another; I cannot possibly answer all of them, one after another.' Indeed he continued to receive such letters until the edition of his works was published in 1851, though the matter was repeatedly discussed and explained in the newspapers. The fact is, that the speech he wrote for John Adams has such an air of truth and reality about it, that only a genius like Mr. Webster, perfectly familiar with whatever relates to the Revolution, and indeed with its spirit, could have written it."

There is hardly a school-boy who reads this book who has not declaimed his famous speech, beginning, 'Sink or swim, live or die, survive or perish, I give my hand and my heart to this vote.' It is hard to believe that this noble and impressive speech, so true to the sturdy character of Mr. Adams, and so appropriate to the occasion, was written by Mr. Webster one morning, before breakfast, in his library. It is also surprising that the orator was not certain whether it really had merit or not, and read it to Mr. Ticknor for his opinion.

Though parts of this speech are familiar, I shall nevertheless conclude my chapter with the exordium, since it will be read with fresh interest in this connection.

"This is an unaccustomed spectacle. For the first time, fellow citizens, badges of mourning shroud the columns and overhang the arches of this hall. These walls, which were consecrated so long ago to the cause of American liberty, which witnessed her infant struggles, and rang with the shouts of her earliest victories, proclaim now that distinguished friends and champions of that great cause have fallen. It is right that it should be thus. The tears which flow and the honors which are paid when the founders of the republic die give hope that the republic itself may be immortal. It is fit that by public assembly and solemn observance, by anthem and by eulogy, we commemorate the services of national benefactors, extol their virtues, and render thanks to God for eminent blessings, early given and long continued, to our favored country.

"Adams and Jefferson are no more, and we are assembled, fellow citizens, the aged, the middle-aged, and the young, by the spontaneous impulse of all, under the authority of the municipal government, with the presence of the chief

magistrate of the commonwealth and others, its
official representatives, the university, and the
learned societies, to bear our part in the manifestations of respect and gratitude which universally pervade the land. Adams and Jefferson
are no more. On our fiftieth anniversary, the
great day of national jubilee, in the very hour of
public rejoicing, in the midst of echoing and reechoing voices of thanksgiving, while their own
names were on all tongues, they took their flight
together to the world of spirits.

"If it be true that no one can safely be pronounced happy while he lives, if that event
which terminates life can alone crown its honor
and its glory, what felicity is here! The great
epic of their lives how happily concluded!
Poetry itself has hardly closed illustrious lives
and finished the career of earthly renown by
such a consummation. If we had the power, we
could not wish to reverse this dispensation of
Divine Providence. The great objects of life
were accomplished, the drama was ready to be
closed. It has closed; our patriots have fallen;
but so fallen, at such age, with such coincidence,
on such a day, that we cannot rationally lament
that that end has come, which we know could not
long be deferred.

"Neither of these great men, fellow citizens.

could have died at any time without leaving an immense void in our American society. They have been so intimately, and for so long a time, blended with the history of the country, and especially so united in our thoughts and recollections with the events of the Revolution, that the death of either would have touched the strings of public sympathy. We should have felt that one great link connecting us with former times was broken; that we had lost something more, as it were, of the presence of the Revolution itself and of the Act of Independence, and were driven on by another great remove from the days of our country's early distinction, to meet posterity and to mix with the future. Like the mariner, whom the ocean and the winds carry along, till he sees the stars which have directed his course and lighted his pathless way descend one by one beneath the rising horizon, we should have felt that the stream of time had borne us onward till another great luminary, whose light had cheered us and whose guidance we had followed, had sunk from our sight.

"But the concurrence of their death on the anniversary of independence has naturally awakened stronger emotions. Both had been presidents, both were early patriots, and both were distinguished and ever honored by their immediate agency in the act of independence. It cannot but seem striking and extraordinary that these two should live to see the fiftieth year from the date of that act; that they should complete that year; and that then, on the day which had just linked forever their own fame with their country's glory, the heavens should open to receive them both at once. As their lives themselves were the gifts of Providence, who is not willing to recognize in their happy termination, as well as in their long continuance, proofs that our country and its benefactors are objects of His care?"

Towards the close of the oration we find a striking passage familiar to many, and justly admired, touching the duties which devolve upon the favored citizens of the United States.

"This lovely land, this glorious liberty, these benign institutions, the dear purchase of our fathers, are ours; ours to enjoy, ours to preserve, ours to transmit. Generations past and generations to come hold us responsible for this sacred trust. Our fathers from behind admonish us with their anxious paternal voices; posterity calls out to us from the bosom of the future; the world turns hither its solicitous eyes; all, all conjure us to act wisely and faithfully in the relation which we sustain.

"We can never, indeed, pay the debt which is upon us; but, by virtue, by morality, by religion, by the cultivation of every good principle and every good habit, we may hope to enjoy the blessing through our day, and to leave it unimpaired to our children. Let us feel deeply how much of what we are, and of what we possess, we owe to this liberty, and to these institutions of government. Nature has indeed given us a soil which yields bounteously to the hands of industry, the mighty and fruitful ocean is before us, and the skies over our heads shed health and vigor. But what are lands, and skies, and seas to civilized man, without society, without knowledge, without morals, without religious culture? and how can these be enjoyed, in all their extent and all their excellence, but under the protection of wise institutions and a free government? Fellow citizens, there is not one of us, there is not one of us here present, who does not at this moment, and every moment, experience in his own condition, and in the condition of those most near and dear to him, the influence and the benefits of this liberty and these institutions. Let us then acknowledge the blessing, let us feel it deeply and powerfully, let us cherish a strong affection for it, and resolve to maintain and perpetuate it. The blood of our fathers, let it not have been shed in vain; the great hope of posterity, let it not be blasted!"

It has been said with truth that no funeral oration has ever been pronounced, in any age, and in any language, which exceeds this in eloquence and simple grandeur. Happy the country that possesses two citizens of whom such praises can be uttered, and happy the nation that can find an orator of such transcendent genius to pronounce their eulogies!

CHAPTER XXVIII.

HOME LIFE AND DOMESTIC SORROWS.

In speaking of Mr. Webster as an orator I have for some time neglected to speak of him in his domestic relations. He was blessed with a happy home. The wife he had chosen was fitted by intellect and culture to sympathize with him in his important work. Moreover, she had those sweet domestic qualities which are required to make home happy. Children had been born to them, and these were an important factor in the happiness of Mr. Webster's home. He had a warm love for children, and was always an affectionate and indulgent parent, seldom chiding, but rebuking in love when occasion required.

In January, 1817, came the first bereavement. His daughter, Grace, always precocious and delicate, developed lung trouble and wasted away. She seems to have been a remarkably bright and attractive child. Her heart was easily touched by sorrow or destitution, and she would never consent that applicants for relief should be sent from the door unsatisfied. "She would bring them herself into the house, see that their wants were supplied, comfort them with the ministration of her own little hands and the tender compassion of her large eyes. If her mother ever refused, those eyes would fill with tears, and she would urge their requests so perseveringly that there was no resisting her."

The death of this sweet child touched Mr. Webster nearly, and it was with a saddened heart that he returned to Washington to devote himself to his duties in the Supreme Court.

On the 18th of December, 1824, death once more appeared in the little household, this time removing the youngest boy, Charles, then nearing his second birthday. This child, young as he was, is said to have borne a closer resemblance to his father than any of his other children. Both parents were devoted to him. Mrs. Webster writes to her husband just after the little boy's death: "It was an inexpressible consolation to me, when I contemplated him in his sickness, that he had not one regret for the past, nor one dread for the future; he was as patient as a lamb during all his sufferings, and they were at last so great I was happy when they were ended. I shall always reflect on his brief life with mournful pleasure, and, I hope, remember with gratitude all the joy he gave me, and it has been great. And, oh, how fondly did I flatter myself it would be lasting!

"'It was but yesterday, my child, thy little heart beat high;
And I had scorned the warning voice that told me thou must die.'"

When Mr. Webster received the intelligence of his loss, he, for the first time in years, indulged in his early fondness for verse, and wrote a few stanzas which have been preserved, though they were intended to be seen only by those near and dear to him. The prevailing thought is a striking one. Here are the verses:

"The staff on which my years should lean
  Is broken ere those years come o'er me;
My funeral rites thou shouldst have seen,
  But thou art in the tomb before me.

"Thou rear'st to me no filial stone,
  No parent's grave with tears beholdest;
Thou art my ancestor—my son!
  And stand'st in Heaven's account the oldest.

"On earth my lot was soonest cast,
  Thy generation after mine;
Thou hast thy predecessor passed,
  Earlier eternity is thine.

"I should have set before thine eyes
  The road to Heaven, and showed it clear;
But thou, untaught, spring'st to the skies,
  And leav'st thy teacher lingering here.

"Sweet seraph, I would learn of thee,
  And hasten to partake thy bliss!
And, oh! to thy world welcome me,
  As first I welcomed thee to this."

But a still heavier bereavement was in store, though it was delayed for some years. In the summer of 1827 the health of Mrs. Webster began to fail, and from that time she steadily declined until on the 21st of January, in the following year she died. Of Mr. Webster's bearing at the funeral, Mr. Ticknor writes: "Mr. Webster came to Mr. George Blake's in Summer Street, where we saw him both before and after the funeral. He seemed completely broken-hearted. At the funeral, when, with Mr. Paige, I was making some arrangements for the ceremonies, we noticed that Mr. Webster was wearing shoes that were not fit for the wet walking of the day, and I went to him and asked him if he would not ride in one of the carriages. 'No,' he said, 'my children and I must follow their mother to the grave on foot. I could swim to Charlestown.' A few minutes afterwards he took Nelson and Daniel in either hand, and walked close to the hearse through the streets to the church in whose crypt the interment took place. It was a touching and solemn sight. He was excessively pale."

It is a striking commentary upon the emptiness

of human honors where the heart is concerned that this great affliction came very soon after Mr. Webster's election to the United State Senate, where he achieved his highest fame and gathered his choicest laurels. We can well imagine that he carried a sad heart to the halls of legislation, and realized how poorly the world's honors compensate the heart for the wounds of bereavement. But Daniel Webster was not a man to suffer sorrow to get the mastery of him. He labored the harder in the service of his country, and found in the discharge of duty his best consolation. If I had room I would like to quote the tribute of Judge Storey to the character of Mr. Webster. I confine myself to one sentence: "Few persons have been more deservedly or more universally beloved; few have possessed qualities more attractive, more valuable or more elevating."

A little over a year later there was a fresh sorrow. Ezekiel Webster, the older brother, between whom and Daniel such warm and affectionate relations had always existed, died suddenly under striking circumstances. He was addressing a jury in the court-house at Concord, N. H., speaking with full force, when, without a moment's warning, "he fell backward, without bending a joint, and, so far as appeared, was dead before his head reached the floor."

He was a man of large ability, though necessarily overshadowed by the colossal genius of his younger brother. It would be too much to expect two Daniel Websters in one family. His death had a depressing effect upon Daniel, for the two had been one in sympathy, and each had rejoiced in the success of the other. Together they had struggled up from poverty, achieved an education and professional distinction, and though laboring in different spheres, for Ezekiel kept aloof from politics, they continued to exchange views upon all subjects that interested either. It is not surprising, in view of his desolate household, and the loss of his favorite brother, that Daniel should write: "I confess the world, at present, has an aspect for me anything but cheerful. With a multitude of acquaintances I have few friends; my nearest intimacies are broken, and a sad void is made in the objects of affection." Yet he was constrained to acknowledge that his life, on the whole, had been "fortunate and happy beyond the common lot, and it would be now ungrateful, as well as unavailing, to repine at calamities, of which, as they are human, I must expect to partake."

I have taken pains to speak of Mr. Webster's home affections, because many, but only those who did not know him, have looked upon him as coldly intellectual, with a grand genius, but deficient in human emotions, when, as a fact, his heart was unusually warm and overflowing with tender sympathy.

CHAPTER XXX.

THE BEGINNING OF A GREAT BATTLE.

When Andrew Jackson became President Mr. Webster found himself an anti administration leader. He was respected and feared, and a plan was formed to break him down and overwhelm him in debate. The champion who was supposed equal to this task was Col. Hayne, of South Carolina, a graceful and forcible speaker, backed by the party in power and by the silent influence of John C. Calhoun, who, as Vice-President, presided over the councils of the Senate.

On the 29th day of December, 1829, an apparently innocent resolution was offered by Mr. Foote, of Connecticut, in the following terms:

"*Resolved*, That the Committee on Public Lands be instructed to inquire into the expediency of limiting for a certain period the sales of the public lands to such lands only as have been heretofore offered for sale and are subject to entry at the minimum price; also, whether the office of Surveyor-General may not

The preferment came to him unsought. Mr. Mills, one of the senators from Massachusetts, who had filled his position acceptably, was drawing near the close of his term, and his failing health rendered his re-election impolitic. Naturally Mr. Webster was thought of as his successor, but he felt that he could hardly be spared from the lower House, where he was the leading supporter of the administration of John Quincy Adams. Levi Lincoln was at that time Governor of Massachusetts, and he too had been urged to become a candidate. Mr. Webster wrote him an urgent letter, in the hope of persuading him to favor this step. From that letter I quote:

"I take it for granted that Mr. E. H. Mills will be no longer a candidate. The question then will be, Who is to succeed him? I need not say to you that you yourself will doubtless be a prominent object of consideration in relation to the vacant place, and the purpose of this communication requires me also to acknowledge that I deem it possible that my name also should be mentioned, more or less generally, as one who may be thought of, among others, for the same situation. . . . . There are many strong personal reasons, and, as friends think, and as I think too, some *public* reasons why I should decline the offer of a seat in the Senate if it should be made to me. Without entering at present into a detail of those reasons, I will say that the latter class of them grow out of the public station which I at present fill, and out of the necessity of increasing rather than of diminishing, in both branches of the National Legislature, the strength that may be reckoned on as friendly to the present administration. . . . . To come, therefore, to the main point, I beg to say that I see no way in which the public good can be so well-promoted as by *your* consenting to go into the Senate.

"This is my own clear and decided opinion; it is the opinion, equally clear and decided, of intelligent and patriotic friends here, and I am able to add that it is also the decided opinion of all those friends elsewhere whose judgment in such matters we should naturally regard. I believe I may say, without violating confidence, that it is the wish, entertained with some earnestness, of our friends at Washington that you should consent to be Mr. Mills's successor."

No one certainly can doubt the absolute sincerity of these utterances. It was, and is, unusual for a representative to resist so earnestly what is considered a high promotion. Mr. Webster was an ambitious man, but he thought that the interests of the country required him to stay where he was, and hence his urgency.

But Gov. Lincoln was no less patriotic. In an elaborate reply to Mr. Webster's letter, from which I have quoted above, he urges that "the deficiency of power in the Senate is the weak point in the citadel" of the administration party. "No individual should be placed there but who was *now* in armor for the conflict, who understood the proper mode of resistance, who personally knew and had measured strength with the opposition, who was familiar with the political interests and foreign relations of the country, with the course of policy of the administration, and who would be prepared at once to meet and decide upon the charter of measures which should be proposed. This, I undertake to say, no *novice* in the national council could do. At least I would not promise to attempt it. I feel deeply that I could not do it successfully. There is no affectation of humility in this, and under such impressions I cannot suffer myself to be thought of in a manner which may make me responsible for great mischief in defeating the chance of a better selection."

I am sure my young readers will agree that this correspondence was highly honorable to both these eminent gentlemen. It is refreshing to turn from the self-sufficient and self-seeking politicians of our own day, most of whom are ready to undertake any responsibilities however large, without, doubt of their own fitness, to the modesty and backwardness of these really great men of fifty years since. In the light of Mr. Webster's great career we must decide that Gov. Lincoln was right in deciding that he should be the next senator from Massachusetts.

At any rate such was the decision arrived at, and in June, 1827, Mr. Webster was elected senator for a period of six years. In due time he took his seat. He was no novice, but a man known throughout the country, and quite the equal in fame of any of his compeers. I suppose no new senator has ever taken his seat who was already a man of such wide fame and national importance as Daniel Webster in 1827. Had James A. Garfield, instead of assuming the Presidency, taken the seat in the Senate to which he had been elected on the fourth of March, 1881, his would have been a parallel case.

Of course there was some curiosity as to the opening speech of the already eminent senator. He soon found a fitting theme. A bill was introduced for the relief of the surviving officers of the Revolution. Such a bill was sure to win the active support of the orator who had delivered the address at Bunker Hill.

Alluding to some objections which had been

made to the principle of pensioning them, Mr. Webster said: "There is, I know, something repulsive and opprobrious in the name of pension. But God forbid that I should taunt them with it. With grief, heartfelt grief, do I behold the necessity which leads these veterans to accept the bounty of their country in a manner not the most agreeable to their feelings. Worn out and decrepid, represented before us by those, their former brothers in arms, who totter along our lobbies or stand leaning on their crutches, I, for one, would most gladly support such a measure as should consult at once their services, their years, their necessities and the delicacy of their sentiments. I would gladly give with promptitude and grace, with gratitude and delicacy, that which merit has earned and necessity demands.

"It is objected that the militia have claims upon us; that they fought at the side of the regular soldiers, and ought to share in the country's remembrance. But it is known to be impossible to carry the measure to such an extent as to embrace the militia, and it is plain, too, that the cases are different. The bill, as I have already said, confines itself to those who served, not occasionally, not temporarily, but permanently; who allowed themselves to be counted on as men who were to see the contest through, last as long as it might; and who have made the phrase "'listing for the war' a proverbial expression, signifying unalterable devotion to our cause, through good fortune and ill fortune, till it reached its close.

"This is a plain distinction; and although, perhaps, I might wish to do more, I see good ground to stop here for the present, if we must stop anywhere. The militia who fought at Concord, at Lexington and at Bunker Hill, have been alluded to in the course of this debate in terms of well-deserved praise. Be assured, sir, there could with difficulty be found a man, who drew his sword or carried his musket at Concord, at Lexington or at Bunker Hill, who would wish you to reject this bill. They might ask you to do more, but never to refrain from doing this. Would to God they were assembled here, and had the fate of this bill in their own hands! Would to God the question of its passage were to be put to them! They would affirm it with a unity of acclamation that would rend the roof of the Capitol!"

This is so much in Mr. Webster's style that, had I quoted it without stating that it was his, I think many of my young readers would have been able to guess the authorship.

CHAPTER XXIX.

CALLED TO THE SENATE.

I HAVE called this biography "From Farm-boy to Senator," because it is as a senator that Daniel Webster especially distinguished himself. At different times he filled the position of Secretary of State, but it was in the Senate Chamber, where he was associated with other great leaders, in especial Clay, Calhoun and Hayne, that he became a great central object of attention and admiration.

Mr. Webster was not elected to the Senate till he had reached the age of forty-five. For him it was a late preferment, and when it came he accepted it reluctantly. Mr. Clay was not yet thirty when he entered the Senate, and Mr. Calhoun was Vice-President before he attained the age of forty-five. But there was this advantage in Mr. Webster's case, that when he joined the highest legislative body in the United States he joined it as a giant, fully armed and equipped not only by nature but by long experience in the lower House of Congress, where he was a leader.

be abolished without detriment to the public interest."

This resolution called forth the celebrated debate in which Mr. Webster demolished the eloquent champion of the South in a speech which will live as long as American history.

Mr. Benton, of Missouri, in an elaborate speech furnished the keynote of the campaign. On Monday, the 18th, he made a speech in which a violent attack was made upon New England, its institutions and its representatives. He was followed by Col. Hayne, who elaborated the comparison drawn between the so-called illiberal policy of New England and the generous policy of the South towards the growing West. He charged the East with a spirit of jealousy and an unwillingness that the West should be rapidly settled, taking the resolution of the senator of Connecticut as his text.

This attack excited surprise, not only by its violence and injustice, but by its suddenness. Mr. Webster shared in the general surprise. It was not long before he was led to suspect that he was aimed at as a well-known defender of New England. At any rate, he rose to reply, but a motion for adjournment cut him off, and he was obliged to wait for the next day before he could have the opportunity. The speech he then made, though not his great speech, was able and deserves notice. He disproved in the clearest manner the charges which had been made against New England, and showed that her policy had been the direct reverse. He dwelt especially upon the part which the Eastern States had in settling the great State of Ohio, which even then contained a population of a million. Upon this point he spoke as follows:

"And here, sir, at the epoch of 1794, let us pause and survey the scene. It is now thirty-five years since that scene actually existed. Let us, sir, look back and behold it. Over all that is now Ohio there then stretched one vast wilderness, unbroken, except by two small spots of civilized culture, the one at Marietta, the other at Cincinnati. At these little openings, hardly a pin's point upon the map, the arm of the frontiersman had leveled the forest and let in the sun. These little patches of earth, themselves almost shadowed by the overhanging boughs of the wilderness, which had stood and perpetuated itself from century to century ever since the Creation, were all that had been rendered verdant by the hand of man. In an extent of hundreds and thousands of square miles no other surface of smiling green attested the presence of civilization. The hunter's path crossed mighty rivers flowing in solitary grandeur, whose sources lay in remote and unknown regions of the wilderness. It struck, upon the north, on a vast inland sea, over which the wintry tempest raged as upon the ocean; all around was bare creation.

"It was a fresh, untouched, unbounded, magnificent wilderness. And, sir, what is it now? Is it imagination only, or can it possibly be fact, that presents such a change as surprises and astonishes us when we turn our eyes to what Ohio now is? Is it reality or a dream that in so short a period as even thirty-five years there has sprung up on the same surface an independent State, with a million of people? A million of inhabitants! An amount of population greater than all the cantons of Switzerland; equal to one third of all the people of the United States when they undertook to accomplish their independence! If, sir, we may judge of measures by their results, what lessons do these facts read us on the policy of the government? What inferences do they not authorize upon the general question of kindness or unkindness? What convictions do they enforce as to the wisdom and ability, on the one hand, or the folly and incapacity on the other, of our general management of Western affairs? For my own part, while I am struck with wonder at the success, I also look with admiration at the wisdom and foresight which originally arranged and prescribed the system for the settlement of the public domain."

Mr. Webster said in conclusion: "The Senate will bear me witness that I am not accustomed to allude to local opinions, nor to compare, nor to contrast, different portions of the country. I have often suffered things to pass, which I might properly enough have considered as deserving a remark, without any observation. But I have felt it my duty on this occasion to vindicate the State which I represent from charges and imputations on her public character and conduct which I know to be undeserved and unfounded. If advanced elsewhere, they might be passed, perhaps, without notice. But whatever is said here is supposed to be entitled to public regard and to deserve public attention; it derives importance and dignity from the place where it is uttered. As a true representative of the State which has sent me here it is my duty, and a duty which I shall fulfill, to place her history and her conduct, her honor and her character, in their just and proper light.

"While I stand here as representative of Massachusetts, I will be her true representative, and, by the blessing of God, I will vindicate her character, motives and history from every imputation coming from a respectable source."

This was the first reply of Webster to Hayne, and it was able and convincing. But Col. Hayne and his friends had no intention of leaving the matter there. The next day the consideration of the bill was renewed. Mr. Webster's friends wished to have the discussion postponed as he had an important case pending in the Supreme Court. Mr. Hayne objected, saying in a theatrical tone, "that he saw the senator from Massachusetts in his seat, and presumed he could make an arrangement that would enable him to be present during the discussion. He was unwilling that the subject should be postponed until he had an opportunity of replying to some of the observations which had fallen from the gentleman yesterday. He would not deny that some things had fallen from the gentleman which rankled here [touching his breast], from which he would desire at once to relieve himself. The gentleman had discharged his fire in the face of the Senate. He hoped he would now afford him the opportunity of returning the shot."

"Then it was," as a Southern member of Congress afterwards expressed it, "that Mr. Webster's person seemed to become taller and larger. His chest expanded and his eyeballs dilated. Fold-ing his arms in a composed, firm and most expressive manner, he exclaimed: 'Let the discussion proceed. I am ready. I am ready *now* to receive the gentleman's fire.'"

Col. Hayne's speech was the great effort of his life. He was a ready, accomplished and forcible speaker, and he vainly thought himself a match for the great senator from Massachusetts whose power he was yet to understand. He spoke as one who was confident of victory, with a self-confidence, a swagger, a violence of invective, which increased as he went on. He was encouraged by the evident delight of his friends, including the Vice-President. He did not finish his speech the first day, but closed with a hint of what he intended to do.

"Sir," he said, "the gentleman from Massachusetts has thought proper, for purposes best known to himself, to strike the South through me, the most unworthy of her servants. He has crossed the border, he has invaded the State of South Carolina, is making war upon her citizens, and endeavoring to overthrow her principles and institutions. Sir, when the gentleman provokes me to such a conflict, I meet him at the threshold, I will struggle while I have life for our altars and our firesides, and if God gives me strength I will drive back the invader discomfited. Nor shall I stop there. If the gentleman provokes war he shall have war. Sir, I will not stop at the border; I will carry the war into the enemy's territory, and not consent to lay down my arms until I shall have obtained 'indemnity for the past and security for the future.' It is with unfeigned reluctance that I enter upon the performance of this part of my duty. I shrink, almost instinctively, from a course, however necessary, which may have a tendency to excite sectional feelings and sectional jealousies. But, sir, the task has been forced upon me, and I proceed right onward to the performance of my duty, be the consequences what they may; the responsibility is with those who have imposed upon me the necessity. The senator from Massachusetts has thought proper to cast the first stone, and, if he shall find, according to a homely adage, that 'he lives in a glass house,' on his head be the consequences."

Brave words these! But brave words do not necessarily win the victory, and Col. Hayne little knew what a foe he was challenging to combat.

CHAPTER XXXI.

THE REPLY TO HAYNE.

BEFORE going farther I must speak of a pestilent doctrine then held in South Carolina, which underlay the whole controversy, and was the animating cause of the antagonism of the Southern leaders to the patriotic representatives of the North. This was known as nullification, and Mr. Calhoun was its sponsor. To explain: South Carolina claimed the right to overrule any law of the general government which did not please her, or which her courts might judge to be unconstitutional. If she did not see fit to pay customs, she claimed that the government could not coerce her. All power was reposed in her own executive, her own legislature, and her own judiciary, and the national power was subordinate to them.

It will be easily seen that this was a most dangerous doctrine to hold, one which if allowed would everywhere subject the national authority to contempt. The United States never had an external foe half so insidious or half so dangerous as this assumption which had grown up within its own borders.

To return to the great debate. When Col. Hayne took his seat at the close of his second speech his friends gathered round him in warm congratulation. Mr. Webster's friends were sober. Much as they admired him, they did not see how he was going to answer that speech. They knew that he would have little or no time for preparation, and it would not do for him to make an ordinary or commonplace reply to such a dashing harangue. So on the evening of Monday the friends of Mr. Webster walked about the streets gloomy and preoccupied. They feared for their champion.

But how was it with him? During Col. Hayne's speech he calmly took notes. Occasionally there was a flash from the depths of his dark eyes as a hint or a suggestion occurred to him, but he seemed otherwise indifferent and unmoved. He spent the evening as usual, and enjoyed a refreshing night's sleep.

In the morning of the eventful day three hours before the hour of meeting crowds set their faces towards the Capitol. At twelve o'clock the Senate Chamber—its galleries, floors and even lobbies—was filled to overflowing. The Speaker retained his place unwillingly in the House, but hardly enough members were present to transact business.

When the fitting time came Mr. Webster rose. He was in the full vigor of a magnificent manhood, the embodiment of conscious strength. He gazed around him, never more self possessed than at that moment. He saw his adversaries with their complacent faces already rejoicing in his anticipated discomfiture; he looked in the faces of his friends, and he noted their looks of anxious solicitude; but he had full confidence in his own strength, and his deep cavernous eyes glowed with "that stern joy which warriors feel in foemen worthy of their steel."

There was a hush of expectation and a breathless silence as those present waited for his first words.

He began thus: "Mr. President, when the mariner has been tossed for many days, in thick weather, and on an unknown sea, he naturally avails himself of the first pause in the storm, the earliest glance of the sun, to take his latitude, and ascertain how far the elements have driven him from his true course. Let us imitate this prudence, and before we float further on the waves of this debate, refer to the point from which we departed, that we may at least be able to form some conjecture where we now are. I ask for the reading of the resolution."

This was felt to be a happy exordium, and was sufficient to rivet the attention of the vast audience.

After the resolution was read Mr. Webster continued: "We have thus heard, sir, what the resolution is which is actually before us for consideration; and it will readily occur to every one that it is almost the only subject about which something has not been said in the speech, running through two days, by which the Senate has been now entertained by the gentleman from South Carolina. Every topic in the wide range of our public affairs, whether past or present, everything, general or local, whether belonging to national politics or party politics, seems to have attracted more or less of the honorable member's attention, save only the resolution before the Senate. He has spoken of everything but the public lands; they have escaped his notice. To that subject in all his excursions he has not paid even the cold respect of a passing glance.

"When this debate, sir, was to be resumed on Thursday morning, it so happened that it would have been convenient for me to be elsewhere. The honorable member however, did not incline to put off the discussion to another day. He had a shot, he said, to return, and he wished to discharge it. That shot, which it was kind thus to inform us was coming, that we might stand out of the way, or prepare ourselves to fall before it and die with decency, has now been received. Under all advantages, and with expectation awakened by the tone which preceded it, it has been discharged and has spent its force. It may become me to say no more of its effect than that, if nobody is found, after all, either killed or wounded by it, it is not the first time in the history of human affairs that the vigor and success of the war have not quite come up to the lofty and sounding phrase of the manifesto."

Referring to Col. Hayne's statement that there was something rankling here (indicating his heart) which he wished to relieve, Mr. Webster said: "In this respect, sir, I have a great advantage over the honorable gentleman. There is nothing *here*, sir, which gives me the slightest uneasiness; neither fear nor anger, nor that which is sometimes more troublesome than either, the consciousness of having been in the wrong. . . . I must repeat, also, that nothing has been received *here* which *rankles* or in any way gives me annoyance. I will not accuse the honorable gentleman of violating the rules of civilized war; I will not say he poisoned his arrows. But whether his shafts were, or were not, dipped in that which would have caused rankling if they had reached, there was not, as it happened, quite strength enough in the bow to bring them to their mark. If he wishes now to gather up these shafts he must look for them elsewhere; they will not be found fixed and quivering in the object at which they were aimed."

Col. Hayne and his friends, as they listened to these words, breathing a calm consciousness of power not unmixed with a grand disdain, must have realized that they had exulted too soon. Indeed Hayne's friends had not all looked forward with confidence to his victory. Senator Iredell, of North Carolina, to a friend of Hayne's who was praising his speech, had said the evening previous, "He has started the lion—but wait till we hear his roar, or feel his claws."

While I do not propose to give an abstract of this famous oration, I shall quote some of the most brilliant and effective passages, well known and familiar though they are, because they will be re-read with fresh and added interest in this connection. There was not a son of Massachusetts, nay, there was not a New Englander, whose heart was not thrilled by the splendid tribute to Massachusetts.

"Mr. President, I shall enter upon no encomium on Massachusetts; she needs none. There she is. Behold her and judge for yourselves. There is her history; the world knows it by heart. The past, at least, is secure. There is Boston, and Concord, and Lexington, and Bunker Hill; and there they will remain forever. The bones of her sons, falling in the great struggle for independence, now lie mingled with the soil of every State from New England to Georgia, and there they will lie forever. And, sir, where American liberty raised its first voice, and where its youth was nurtured and sustained, there it still lives, in the strength of its manhood and full of its original spirit. If discord and disunion shall wound it, if party strife and blind ambition shall hawk at and tear it, if folly and madness, if uneasiness under salutary and necessary restraint, shall succeed in separating it from that union by which alone its existence is made sure, it will stand, in the end, by the side of that cradle in which its infancy was rocked; it will stretch forth its arm with whatever of vigor it may still retain over the friends who gather round it; and it will fall at last, if fall it must, amidst the proudest monuments of its own glory, and on the very spot of its origin."

Mr. Webster shows his magnanimity by pronouncing, in like manner, an eulogium upon his opponent's native State, which is in bright contrast with the mean and unjust attacks of Col. Hayne upon Massachusetts. This is what he says:

"Let me observe that the eulogium pronounced on the character of South Carolina by the honorable gentleman for her Revolutionary and other merits meets my hearty concurrence. I shall not acknowledge that the honorable member goes before me in regard for whatever of distinguished talent, of distinguished character, South Carolina has produced. I claim part of the honor. I partake in the pride of her great names. I claim them for countrymen, one and all, the Laurenses, the Rutledges, the Pinkneys, the Sumters, the Marions, Americans all, whose fame is no more to be hemmed in by State lines than their talents and patriotism were capable of being circumscribed within the same narrow limits. In their day and generation they served and honored the country, and the whole country; and their renown is one of the treasures of the whole country. Him whose honored name the gentleman himself bears—does he esteem me less capable of gratitude for his patriotism, or sympathy for his sufferings, than if his eyes had first opened upon the light of Massachusetts instead of South Carolina? Sir, does he suppose it is his power to exhibit a Carolina name so bright as to produce envy in my bosom? No, sir; increased gratification rather. I thank God that, if I am gifted with little of the spirit which is able to raise mortals to the skies, I have yet none, as I trust, of that other spirit which would drag angels down. When I shall be found, sir, in my place here in the Senate, or elsewhere, to sneer at public merit because it happens to spring up beyond the little limits of my own State or neighborhood; when I refuse, for any such cause, or for any cause, the homage due to American talent, to elevated patriotism, to sincere devotion to liberty and the country; or, if I see an uncommon endowment of Heaven, if I see extraordinary capacity and virtue in any son of the South, and if, moved by local prejudice or gangrened by State jealousy, I get up here to abate the tithe of a hair from his just character and just fame, may my tongue cleave to the roof of my mouth!"

It must not be supposed that Mr. Webster's speech was merely of a personal character. In a sound and logical manner he discussed the limits of constitutional authority, and combated the pernicious doctrine of State supremacy, which thirty years later was to kindle a civil war of vast proportions, the starting-point being South Carolina. At the risk of quoting paragraphs which my young readers may skip, I proceed to introduce an extract which may give an idea of this part of the oration.

"We approach at length, sir, to a more important part of the honorable gentleman's observations. Since it does not accord with my views of justice and policy to give away the public lands altogether, as mere matter of gratuity, I am asked by the honorable gentleman on what ground it is that I consent to vote them away in particular instances. How, he inquires, do I reconcile with these profound sentiments my support of measures appropriating portions of the land to particular roads, particular canals, particular rivers, and particular institutions of education in the West ? This leads, sir, to the real and wide difference in political opinion between the honorable gentleman and myself. On my part, I look upon all these objects as connected with the common good, fairly embraced in its object and terms; he, on the contrary, deems them all, if good at all, only local good.

"This is our difference.

"The interrogatory which he proceeded to put at once explains this difference. 'What interest,' asks he, 'has South Carolina in a canal in Ohio?'

Sir, this very question is full of significance. It develops the gentleman's whole political system, and its answer expounds mine. Here we differ. I look upon a road over the Alleghanies, a canal round the Falls of the Ohio, or a canal or railway from the Atlantic to the Western waters, as being an object large and extensive enough to be fairly said to be for the common benefit. The gentleman thinks otherwise, and this is the key to his construction of the powers of the government. He may well ask what interest has South Carolina in a canal in Ohio. On his system, it is true, she has no interest. On that system, Ohio and South Carolina are different governments and different countries; connected here, it is true, by some slight and ill-defined bond of union, but in all main respects separate and diverse. On that system South Carolina has no more interest in a canal in Ohio than in Mexico. The gentleman, therefore, only follows out his own principles; he does no more than arrive at the natural conclusions of his own doctrines; he only announces the true results of that creed which he has adopted himself, and would persuade others to adopt, when he thus declares that South Carolina has no interest in a public work in Ohio.

"Sir, we narrow-minded people of New England do not reason thus. Our notion of things is entirely different. We look upon the States not as separated but united. We love to dwell on that union, and on the mutual happiness which it has so much promoted, and the common renown which it has so greatly contributed to acquire. In our contemplation South Carolina and Ohio are parts of the same country, States united under the same general government, having interests common, associated, intermingled. In whatever is within the proper sphere of the constitutional power of this government we look upon the States as one. We do not impose geographical limits to our patriotic feelings or regard; we do not follow rivers and mountains and lines of latitude to find boundaries beyond which public improvements do not benefit us.

"We who come here, as agents and representatives of these narrow-minded and selfish men of New England, consider ourselves as bound to regard with an equal eye the good of the whole in whatever is within our power of legislation. Sir, if a railroad or canal, beginning in South Carolina and ending in South Carolna, appeared to me to be of national importance and national magnitude, believing, as I do, that the power of government extends the encouragement of works of that description, if I were to stand up here and ask, What interest has Massachusetts in a railroad in South Carolina? I should not be willing to face my constituents. These same narrow-minded men would tell me that they had sent me to act for the whole country, and that one who possessed too little comprehension either of intellect or feeling, one who was not large enough both in mind and in heart to embrace the whole, was not fit to be intrusted with the interests of our part."

This will give an idea of the broad national sentiments entertained and expressed by the senator from Massachusetts. It is certainly in strong contrast to the narrow sectional views of Col. Hayne and John C. Calhoun.

Towards the close of his speech Mr. Webster describes in an amusing way a supposed conflict in South Carolina between the customs officers of the government and a local force led by his opponent. It was playful, but Col. Hayne was moved by the ridicule with which it covered him more than by any of Mr. Webster's arguments.

It need hardly be said that the entire address was listened to with rapt attention. As it proceeded, those friends of Mr. Webster who doubted his ability to cope with the Southern champion, and who had listened to his first words with feelings of anxious solicitude, became cheerful and even jubilant. In fact, they changed aspects with Hayne's friends who had awaited the opening of the speech with supercilious disdain. The calm power, the humorous contempt, with which Mr. Webster handled the doughty champiiona nnoyed them not a little.

I do not mean to underrate the aiblity or eloquence of Col. Hayne. Upon this point it is sufficient to quote the opinion of Mr. Everett, the tried and intimate friend of Daniel Webster, who says: "It is unnecessary to state, except to those who have come forward quite recently, that Col. Hayne was a gentleman of ability very far above the average, a highly accomplished debater, an experienced politician, a person possessing the full confidence of his friends, and entirely familiar with the argument on which the theory controverted in Mr. Webster's speech rests."

Mr. March, in his "Reminiscences of Congress," a

book from which I have received valuable help in the composition of this chapter, describes Hayne's oratory in these terms:

"Hayne dashed into debate like the Mameluke cavalry upon a charge. There was a gallant air about him that could not but win admiration. He never provided for retreat; he never imagined it. He had an invincible confidence in himself, which arose partly from constitutional temperament, partly from previous success. His was the Napoleonic warfare: to strike at once for the capital of the enemy, heedless of danger or cost to his own forces. Not doubting to overcome all odds, he feared none, however seemingly superior. Of great fluency and no little force of expression, his speech never halted, and seldom fatigued."

Mr. Webster swept on to the close of his speech with power unabated. Some of his friends had feared he could not sustain his elevated flight, that he would mar the effect of his great passages by dropping to the commonplace. They had no need to fear. He thorouglhy understood his own powers. At length he reached the peroration—that famous peroration, so well known, yet, in spite of its familiarity, so impossible to omit here.

"When my eyes shall be turned to behold for the last time the sun in heaven, may I not see him shining on the broken and dishonored fragments of a once glorious Union; on States dissevered, discordant, belligerent; on a land rent with civil feuds, or drenched, it may be, in fraternal blood! Let their last feeble and lingering glance rather behold the gorgeous ensign of the republic, now known and honored throughout the earth, still full high advanced, its arms and trophies streaming in their original luster, not a stripe erased or polluted, not a single star obscured, bearing for its motto no such miserable interrogatory, 'What is all this worth?' nor those other words of delusion and folly, 'Liberty first and Union afterwards;' but everywhere, spread all over in characters of living light, blazing on all its ample folds, as they float over the seas and over the land, and in every wind under the whole heavens, that other sentiment, dear to every American heart—Liberty and Union, now and forever, one and inseparable!"

Hayne attempted a reply to this speech, but it had little effect. It was followed by a telling *resume* of his positions by Mr. Webster, and so far as these two speakers were concerned the discussion closed.

It is remarkable how little effort this famous oration cost its author. The constitutional argument, to be sure, was familiar to him, and he had but to state it, but for the great passages, including the exordium, the peroration, the encomium upon Massachusetts, the speaker was indebted to the inspiration of the moment; yet they are so compact, so fitly expressed, so elegantly worded, that he would be a bold man who should suggest even a verbal change.

CHAPTER XXXII.

THE SECRET OF WEBSTER'S POWER.

It is hardly necessary to say that when Mr. Webster's speech in reply to Hayne was published and read by the country at large it made a profound impression. Doubtess, it kindled afresh in many wavering hearts a love for that Union the claims of which upon the American citizen the orator so strongly urged. It is interesting to know that Hayne himself, while he essayed to answer it, appreciated its power.

Mr. Harvey relates, upon Mr. Webster's authority, that when he had finished his speech some Southern members approached him cordially and said, "Mr. Webster, I think you had better die now and rest your fame on that speech."

Mr. Hayne, who was standing near by, and heard the remark, said, "You ought not to die; a man who can make such speeches as that ought never to die."

It is related that Mr. Webster, meeting his opponent at the President's reception the same evening, went up to him and remarked pleasantly:

"How are you to-night?"

"None the better for you, sir," answered Hayne, humorously.

Henry Clay wrote later: "I congratulate you on the very great addition which you have made during the session to your previous high reputation. Your speeches, and particularly in reply to Mr. Hayne, are the theme of praise from every tongue, and I have shared in the delight which all have felt."

In its powerful defense of the Constitution Mr. Webster carried with him patriotic men all over the country. Hon. William Gaston, of North Carolina, wrote thus: "The ability with which the great argument is treated, the patriotic fervor with which the Union is asserted, give you claim to the gratitude of every one who loves his country and regards the Constitution as its best hope and surest stay. My engrossing occupations leave me little leisure for any correspondence except on business, but I have resolved to seize a moment to let you know that with us there is scarcely a division of opinion among the intelligent portion of the community. All of them whose understanding or whose conscience is not surrendered to the servitude of faction, greet your eloquent efforts with unmixed gratification."

It is an interesting question how far Mr. Webster prepared himself for this his greatest, or, at any rate, his most effective parliamentary speech.

Upon this point let us read the statement of Mr. Webster himself, as given to his tried friend, Mr. Harvey.

In reference to the remark that he had made no preparation for the Hayne speech, he said: "That was not quite so. If it was meant that I took notes and studied with a view to a reply, that was not true; but that I was thoroughly conversant with the subject of debate, from having made preparation for a totally different purpose than that speech, is true. The preparation for my reply to Hayne was made upon the occasion of Mr. Foote's resolution to sell the public lands. Some years before that, Mr. McKinley, a senator from Alabama, introduced a resolution into the Senate, proposing to cede the public domains to the States in which they were situated

It struck me at that time as being so unfair and improper that I immediately prepared an argument to resist it. My argument embraced the whole history of the public lands, and the government's action in regard to them. Then there was another question involved in the Hayne debate. It was as to the right and practice of petiton. Mr. Calhoun had denied the right of petition on the subject of slavery. In other words, he claimed that if the petition was for some subject which the Senate had no right to grant, then there was no right of petition. If the Senate had no such right, then the petitioners had no right to come there. Calhoun's doctrine seemed to be accepted, and I made preparation to answer his proposition. It so happened that the debate did not take place, because the matter never was pressed. I had my notes tucked away in a pigeon-hole, and when Hayne made that attack upon me and upon New England I was already posted, and only had to take down my notes and refresh my memory. In other words, if he had tried to make a speech to fit my notes he could not have hit it better. No man is inspired with the occasion; I never was."

Mr. Webster was too great a man to wish for praise which he did not deserve. That is for men of inferior ability, who are glad to have it believed that their most elaborate utterances are "thrown off upon the spur of the moment." Indeed, he does not claim enough when he disclaims being inspired by the occasion. His encomium upon New England, his glowing peroration, were fused and put into enduring form under the pressure of strong emotion, which may well be termed inspiration. Yet it was always his habit to ascribe his great efforts to hard labor rather than to genius, and he remarked to a young clergyman on one occasion, who had questioned him in regard to some of his speeches, "Young man, there is no such thing as extemporaneous acquisition."

If a man like Daniel Webster felt constrained to say this, how much more ought labor to be held necessary by the ordinary mind. My young readers may be assured that diligent and uncomplaining toil are the secret springs in most cases of worldly success.

So, if they chance to dash off a smooth esay in as mood of inspiration, they may have good cause to doubt whether it has any solid value. I recall a certain school where a prize was offered for an essay on a subject requiring a certain amount of thought and research. The leading contestants were two boys, one quick and brilliant, the other slow and plodding, but sound. Both were anxious to succeed. The second began in due time and worked steadily, not allowing himself to be unduly hurried. The first waited till within two days of the date at which the essays were to be submitted, and then dashed off an essay which was very creditable under the circumstances. But it did not win. It was slow and sure that won the prize, then, as in so many other cases. I am glad to have the potent example of Daniel Webster to help me in enforcing a lesson so valuable to youth.

Yet Mr. Webster was always ready of speech. He could make a great speech upon any occasion, and upon any subject, however slight. An illustration of this is given by Hon. John Wentworth, of Illinois, in a letter from which I proceed to quote:

"Mr. Webster won my lasting gratitude by his assistance in the passage of the River and Harbor bill, in 1846. The bill had passed the House and been referred to the Committee on Commerce, a majority of whom were of the 'strict construction' school, believing that Congress could improve a natural harbor, but could not make one. I went before the committee to defend the appropriation for a harbor at Little Fort, now called Waukegan. I found I had no friends there but Senator Reverdy Johnson, of Maryland. The committee recommended that the appropriation be struck out. Senator John A. Dix, of New York, led the opposition. He had been a graduate of West Point, was a good engineer, had brought the map of survey into the Senate, and was having great influence against it. I was seated in the lobby directly behind Col. Thomas H. Benton, and Webster was upon his usual walk. He gave me a nod of recognition and passed on. Gen. Dix kept up his fire, and I felt it. Our senators, Sidney Breese and James Semple, were both from the southern part of our State, and had no personal knowledge of the merits of the case. The Indiana senators were similarly situated. Wisconsin had no senators. And the Michigan senators lived at Detroit, and they had only a general knowledge of Lake Michigan.

"As Webster was traveling to and fro past me, the thought occurred to me that, as he was 'a liberal constructionist,' he was just the man to rectify all the damage that Gen. Dix was doing. But it was a small matter for so great a man. Besides, I knew that his colleague, Senator John Davis, was taking the side of Gen. Dix. As Webster would pass me I would resolve that the next time he would come I would speak to him. But my courage would forsake me when I reflected that he was a Whig and I was a Democrat. I wanted some excuse to speak to him. He had known my father. He was a son of New Hampshire, and a graduate of the same college with myself. But my heart failed me; and yet it was all the while sighing, 'Webster, Webster, do but speak to me.'

"At length came his voice, in deep, sepulchral tone, 'Wentworth, what is Dix making all this ado about?'

"Promptly the answer came: 'Mr. Webster, since your trip around the lakes from Chicago, in 1837, we have had but few appropriations for old harbors and none for new ones. This place is half way between Chicago and Milwaukee, and we want a harbor of refuge there.'

"'I see the point, I see the point,' says Webster, and at once went to his seat upon the Senate floor.

"When Gen. Dix had concluded, Mr. Webster observed that he could add nothing to the conclusive argument of the senator from New York in favor of the appropriation. He thought he had satisfied all the senators that there was no harbor at the place, and so the House must have thought when it made the appropriation to construct one there. Upon what did the senator from New York found his doctrine that, when God created the world, or even Lake Michigan, He left nothing for man to do? The curse pronounced upon our first parents for their transgression was in entire conflict with any such doctrine. He did not believe that the Constitution of the United States was such a narrowly contracted instrument that it would not permit the construction of a harbor where the necessities of commerce required it. He then foreshadowed the growth of the West, its abundant products, its gigantic commerce, its numerous people. He started a steamer from Chicago laden to the guards with freight and passengers. He then described a storm in a manner that no man but Webster could describe. His flight of eloquence equaled his best at Bunker Hill or Plymouth Rock. You could hear the dashing waves, the whistling winds, the creaking timbers, and the shrieking passengers, and, as he sent the vessel to the bottom with all on board, he exclaimed: 'What but a merciful Providence saved me from such a catastrophe when I passed over Lake Michigan in 1837?' At such a dire disaster could the senator from New York derive any consolation from the reflection that his narrow interpretation of the Constitution had been maintained?

"As Webster closed Col. Benton turned to me and said, 'That is the greatest speech upon so small a matter that I ever heard.' Reverdy Johnson came up and said, 'Now, don't you abuse the Whigs any more.' And Senator Breese said, 'Now you can go back to the House. That speech saves us.'

"The bill passed without amendment. But alas! President Polk vetoed it. And out of his veto grew that wonderful event in the history of Chicago, the river and harbor convention of 1847, a vast assemblage, composed of the most talented, enterprising, wealthy and influential men of all parts of the country. At the laying of the corner stone of the Douglas Monument, Gen. Dix was here as the principal orator. While others were speaking, I called his attention to our magnificent harbor works. After complimenting them highly he said, 'They ought to protect you from any storm—even from such a one as Webster manufactured for you in the Senate in 1846.'"

It must be remembered that this readiness of Mr. Webster arose not wholly from his great powers, but largely from the fact that all his life long he had been a diligent and faithful student. Hence it was that his mind was a vast reservoir of acquisition from which he could at will draw out what was most fitting upon any subject. So Sir Walter Scott, browsing in his boyhood among the treasures of legendry lore and feudal traditions, was unconsciously preparing himself for the novels and poetical romances with which many years afterwards he delighted the world, and made his native land famous.

Recurring to the subject of nullification, at which Mr. Webster had aimed so powerful a blow, it may be said that it was scotched but not killed. Col. Hayne was overwhelmed, but he was not convinced. Neither was John C. Calhoun, the greater representative of the same State, who entirely accorded with Hayne in his extreme views of the rights and powers of the separate States. Not long afterwards Col. Hayne resigned his seat in the Senate in order to be elected Governor of South Carolina, and lead at home the opponents of the government, while Mr. Calhoun, resigning his place as Vice-President, was elected senator in the place of Hayne, to lead the forces of nullification on the floor of the Senate. Through the firmness of President Jackson, their schemes came to naught, but were revived, as we know, thirty years later by the citizens of the same State, and the Civil War was the result.

CHAPTER XXXIII.

HONORS RECEIVED IN ENGLAND.

It would require a volume far larger than the present to speak in detail of Mr. Webster's public life, to point out his public services, to enumerate the occasions on which he took a distinguished part in debate. But this does not come within my plan. Fortunately, there are other works in which such as desire it can gain all the information they desire upon these points. They will find how closely Mr. Webster was identified with the history of the nation, and what a powerful influence he exerted upon all public measures. And all the while he was making an equally brilliant reputation at the bar. He was employed in numerous "great cases," and in none was he found unequal to his opportunity.

The result of his multifarious and exhausting labors was a determination to make a tour of recreation, and not unnaturally he decided to visit England, a country which to every American of Anglo-Saxon race must possess a first attraction. His second wife, who died but a few weeks since, his daughter, and Mrs. Page, the wife of his brother-in-law, were of the party. His youngest son, Edward, then a Dartmouth student, joined them later.

Mr. Webster's fame had preceded him, and he received unusual honors. One paper, in announcing his arrival, said, "We cordially welcome to our shores this great and good man, and accept him as a fit representative of all the great and good qualities of our transatlantic brethren." So great was the curiosity to see Him that the press of carriages about the door of his hotel was almost unprecedented. He was invited everywhere, and was cordially received by the most prominent men. In fact, he was a "lion," and that in a marked sense.

Among others, he met that eccentric and craggy genius, Thomas Carlyle, and I am sure my readers young and old will like to know what impression the great senator made upon the Scotch philosopher.

This is what Carlyle writes:

"American notabilities are daily becoming notable among us, the ties of the two parishes, mother and daughter, getting closer and closer knit. Indissoluble ties!

"I reckon that this huge smoky wen may for some centuries yet be the best Mycale for our Saxon Panionium, a yearly meeting place of 'all the Saxons' from beyond the Atlantic, from the antipodes, or wherever the restless wanderers dwell and toil. After centuries, if Boston, if New York, have become the most convenient 'All-Saxondom,' we will right cheerfully go thither to hold such festival and leave the wen.

"Not many days ago I saw at breakfast the notablest

of all your notabilities, Daniel Webster. He is a magnificent specimen. You might say to all the world, 'This is our Yankee Englishman; such limbs we make in Yankee-land!' As a logic-fencer, advocate or parliamentary Hercules, one would incline to back him at first sight against the extant world. The tanned complexion, that amorphous crag-like face, the dull black eyes under the precipice of brows (I am sure no one ever called Mr. Webster's eyes dull before or since), like dull anthracite furnaces only waiting to be *blown*, the mastiff mouth accurately closed—I have not traced so much of *silent Berseker's rage* that I remember of in any other man. 'I guess I should not like to be your nigger.' Webster is not loquacious, but he is pertinent, conclusive, a dignified, perfectly-bred man, though not English in breeding, a man worthy of the best reception among us, and meeting such, I understand."

In a letter to Mr. Ticknor, John Kenyon indulges in some reminiscences of Mr. Webster, whom he met intimately, having traveled with him and his family party during four days.

"Coleridge used to say that he had seldom known or heard of any great man who had not 'much of the woman in him.' Even so, that large intellect of Daniel Webster seemed to be coupled with all softer feelings, and his countenance and bearing at the very first impressed me with this.

"All men, without having studied either science, are, we all know, more or less phrenologists and physiognomists. Right or wrong, I had found as I thought much sensibility in Webster's countenance. A few weeks afterwards I had an opportunity of learning that it was not there only. We were in a hackney coach, driving along the New Road to Baring's in the city. It was a longish drive, and we had time to get into a train of talk, also we were by that time what I may presume to call 'intimate.' I said, 'Mr. Webster, you once, I believe, had a brother?' 'Yes,' he kindly said, 'when I see you and your brother together I often think of him,' and—I speak the fact as it was—I saw, after a little more talk on the subject of his brother, the tears begin to trickle down his cheek till he said to me, 'I'll give you an account of my early life,' and he began with his father, and the farm in New Hampshire, and his own early education, and that of his brother, the details of his courtship and first marriage, and his no property at the time, but of his hopes in his profession and of his success, as he spoke showing much emotion. How could one help loving a man at once so powerful and so tender?"

The opinions of those who are themselves eminent are of interest. Let us see, therefore, what Hallam, the historian, says of our subject.

"I have had more than one opportunity," he writes to Mr. Ticknor, "of hearing of you, especially from your very distinguished countryman, Mr. Webster, with whom I had the pleasure of becoming acquainted last summer. It is but an echo of the common novice here to say that I was extremely struck by his appearance, deportment and conversation. Mr. Webster approaches as nearly to the *beau ideal* of a republican senator as any man that I have ever seen in the course of my life, worthy of Rome or Venice, rather than of our noisy and wrangling generation. I wish that some of our public men here would take example from his grave and prudent manner of speaking on political subjects, which seemed to me neither too incautious nor too strikingly reserved."

It is seldom that a man's personal appearance is so impressive as that of Daniel Webster, seldom that his greatness is so visibly stamped upon his face and figure. An admirer of Mr. Webster was once shocked by hearing him called "a humbug." "What do you mean?" he demanded angrily. "I mean this," was the reply, "that no man can possibly be as great as he looks."

I have said that Mr. Webster was the recipient of attentions from all classes, I may add, from the highest in the land. Mr. and Mrs. Webster dined privately with Queen Victoria by special invitation, and it is recorded that the young queen, for she was then young, was much impressed by the majestic demeanor of the great American. Even the Eton boys, who are wont to chaff all visitors, forgot their propensity in the presence of Mr. Webster. As Mr. Kenyon, already quoted, writes: "Not one look of unseemly curiosity, much less of the quizzing which I had rather anticipated, had we to undergo. Webster was not merely gratified, he was visibly touched by the sight. You remember that Charles Lamb said at Eton—I do not pretend to quote his exact words—'What a pity that these fine youths should grow up into paltry members of Parliament!' For myself, when I saw them so cheerful and yet so civilized and well-conditioned, I remember thinking to myself at the moment, 'Well, if I had a boy I should send him to Eton.'"

While at the Castle Inn, in Windsor, Mr. Webster wrote the following autograph, by request, for Mr. Kenyon:

"When you and I are dead and gone
This busy world will still jog on,
And laugh and sing and be as hearty
As if we still were of the party."

There is no doubt that Mr. Webster enjoyed heartily his well-earned recreation. He had good cause. Never certainly up to that time had an American been received in England with such distinguished honors. I will close by his own account of the way in which he was received.

"I must say that the good people have treated me with great kindness. Their hospitality is unbounded, and I find nothing cold or stiff in their manners, at least not more than is observed among ourselves. There may be exceptions, but I think I may say this as a general truth. The thing in England most prejudiced against the United States is the press. Its ignorance of us is shocking, and it is increased by such absurdities as the travelers publish, to which stock of absurdities I am sorry to say Captain Marryatt is making an abundant addition. In general, the Whigs know more and think better of America than the Tories. This is undeniable. Yet my intercourse I think is as much with the Conservatives as the Whigs. I have several invitations to pass time in the country after Parliament is prorogued. Two or three of them I have agreed to accept. Lord Lansdowne and the

Earl of Radnor have invited us, who live in the south, the Duke of Rutland, Sir Henry Halford, Earl Fitzwilliam, Lord Lonsdale, etc., who live in the north."

Of one thing my young reader may be assured, that no attentions, however elevated the source, had any effect upon the simple dignity of a typical American citizen, or influenced him when a few years later, as Secretary of State, it became his duty to deal with our relations with England.

CHAPTER XXXIV.

CALLED TO THE CABINET.

In the Presidential campaign of 1840, General Harrison, the nominee of the Whig party, swept the country, and was elected amid demonstrations of popular enthusiasm till then unprecedented. As we look back upon this time, uninfluenced by passion, we can only wonder how a man so moderately fitted for the position should have aroused such a furor. That he should have been nominated, while such born leaders and accomplished statesmen as Mr. Webster were passed over, need excite no surprise. In an ideal republic the best man and the wisest statesman would be selected, but there are no ideal statesmen, and are not likely to be. General Harrison was available, and therefore was put forward as the standard bearer.

I do not mean to say that our nominees have always been mediocre men. James A. Garfield was a trained and experienced statesman, so was James Buchanan (his faults were of a different order), so were the early Presidents, and so have been occasional nominees of both great parties; but, as a rule, public men of the first rank have been passed by for candidates more available.

General Harrison showed this evidence of fitness for his high station, that almost immediately after his election, he indicated a strong desire that Mr. Webster should enter his Cabinet. Modestly distrustful of his own abilities, he wished to strengthen his administration by calling to his councils Mr. Webster and Mr. Clay. He writes thus to Mr. Webster, Dec. 1, 1840:

"Since I was first a candidate for the Presidency, I had determined, if successful, to sollicit your able assistance in conducting the administration, and I now ask you to accept the State or Treasury Department. I have myself no preference of either for you, but it may perhaps be more difficult to fill the latter than the former, if you should decline it. It was the first designed for you, in the supposition that you had given more attention to the subject of the finances than Mr. Clay, to whom I intended to have offered the State Department. This, as well as any other post in the Cabinet, I understood, before my arrival here, from an intimate friend of that gentleman, he would decline. This he has done since personally to me."

Mr. Webster replied that "for the daily details of the Treasury, the matters of account, and the supervision of subordinate officers employed in the collection and disbursement of public moneys," he did not think himself to be particularly well qualified. He indicated that he would accept the office of Secretary of State.

Mr. Webster no doubt accurately gauged his own abilities. No one could be better fitted for the premiership and the conduct of our foreign relations, as the event proved. At this time especially a strong, judicious statesman of the first rank was required, for the relations between the United States and Great Britain were very delicate and even critical, and a rash hand might easily have plunged the two countries into war. One vexed question related to the boundary between this country and the provinces of Nova Scotia and Canada. This question was complicated by others of a still more irritating character, which space will not allow me to particularize. There was another question also, the long-standing claim of England to impress her own seamen, and to take them out of American vessels sailing on the high seas in time of war, rendering necessary the odious "right of search."

Mr. Webster was influenced to accept the post of

Secretary of State because he knew these questions ought to be settled, and he felt confident of his ability to settle them. With this view the people cordially agreed, and Gen. Harrison's choice of the great statesman of New England to take charge of our foreign relations was a very popular one.

Mr. Webster's retirement from the Senate, and the necessary choice of a successor, gave occasion for a display of magnanimity. His relations with ex-President John Quincy Adams were not friendly—he felt that he had been very badly treated by Mr. Adams on one occasion—but Mr. Adams, from his prominent position, was likely to be thought of as his successor in the Senate. Upon this subject Mr. Webster writes to a friend: "Some years ago, as you well know, an incident occurred which interrupted intercourse between Mr. Adams and myself for several years, and wounded the feelings of many of my friends as well as my own. With me that occurrence is overlooked and forgotten. I bury all remembrance of it under my regard for Mr. Adams's talents, character and public services. . . . Mr. Adams's great knowledge and ability, his experience, and especially his thorough acquaintance with the foreign relations of the country, will undoubtedly make him prominent as a candidate; and I wish it to be understood that his election would be altogether agreeable to me."

Mr. Adams, however, remained in the House of Representatives, and Rufus Choate was selected to succeed Mr. Webster. Massachusetts was fortunate in having three citizens so eminently fitted to do her honor in the national councils.

When the letter announcing Mr. Webster's resignation of his seat was read in the Senate, Mr. Clay took occasion to pay a glowing tribute to his great eloquence and ability, referring to him as "one of the noblest specimens of American eloquence; one of the brightest ornaments of these halls, of this country, and of our common nature."

The lamented death of General Harrison, on the 5th of April, after but a single month in office, interrupted official business, and made Mr. Webster's position still more difficult. John Tyler, Vice-President, succeeding, soon made himself obnoxious to the party that had elected him. All the members of the Cabinet, except Mr. Webster, resigned. Mr. Webster perceived that he could not do so without serious detriment to the national interests, and he remained steadfast, thereby incurring the censure of many, who did not appreciate the patriotism and self-sacrifice that actuated him. The Secretary of State was too astute a politician not to understand that he was periling his own political fortunes, that he was raising up for himself enemies in his own State, and that his adherence to the administration might cost him the promotion which he ardently desired, for he had already fixed his eyes upon the Presidency as an object to which he might legitimately aspire. Nevertheless, he adhered and kept his post till his work was done, and he had accomplished for this country what no other hand could probably have done, the peaceful adjustment of her foreign differences.

In the midst of the dissatisfaction a great meeting was held at Faneuil Hall, and Mr. Webster determined to go there and face the anger of his former friends. Whatever might have been the feelings of the packed audience when Mr. Webster rose before them in his magnificent manhood, and his deep, calm eyes fell upon the audience, every head was instantly uncovered in involuntary homage.

In the course of his speech Mr. Webster said: "There are always delicacy and regret when one feels obliged to differ from his friends, but there is no embarrassment. There is no embarrassment, because, if I see the path of duty before me, I have that within me which will enable me to pursue it, and throw all embarrassment to the winds. A public man has no occasion to be embarrassed if he is honest. Himself and his feelings should be to him as nobody and as nothing; the interest of his country must be to him as everything; he must sink what is personal to himself, making exertions for his country, and it is his ability and readiness to do this which are to mark him as a great or as a little man in time to come.

"There were many persons in September, 1841, who found great fault with my remaining in the President's Cabinet. You know, gentlemen, that twenty years of honest and not altogether undistinguished service in the Whig cause did not save me from an outpouring of wrath which seldom proceeds from Whig pens and Whig tongues against anybody. I am, gentlemen, a little hard to coax, but as to being driven, this is out of the question. I chose to trust my own judgment; and thinking I was at a post where I was in the service of the country, and could do it good, I stayed there, and I leave it to you to-day to say, I leave it to my countrymen to say, whether the country would have been better off if I had left also. I have no attachment to office. I have tasted of its sweets, but I have tasted of its bitterness. I am content with what I have achieved; I am ready to rest satisfied with what is gained rather than to run the risk of doubtful efforts for new acquisitions."

This is the speech of a strong man—a man not to be turned by obloquy from any step which he has made up his mind to take. I think to-day few would question the good judgment which he displayed in retaining his seat in the Cabinet. He was enabled to negotiate a treaty with Great Britain—known as the Ashburton treaty—which, if not wholly satisfactory to the United States, at any rate harmonized differences to a large extent and removed any immediate danger of hostilities.

When Mr. Webster felt that his work was fully accomplished, on the 8th of May, 1843, he resigned the premiership, and hastened to his seaside home at Marshfield, there to enjoy the rest which he needed and craved.

CHAPTER XXXV.

LIFE AT MARSHFIELD.

The town of Marshfield is as intimately associated with the name of Daniel Webster as is Abbotsford with Sir Walter Scott. It is a sparsely settled town on the southeastern shore of Massachusetts. Mr. Webster's first acquaintance with it dates from 1824. Both

Mr. and Mrs. Webster were charmed with the situation of the Thomas Farm, as it was then called, and the grand views which it afforded of the ocean. For several summers the Websters were boarders in the family of Captain Thomas, and finally, in 1831, he became the owner of the farm by purchase. Then he began to make improvements, and by the lavish expenditure of money converted it from a homely farm to a fitting residence for a famous lawyer.

Henceforth this was the home to which the thoughts of the great statesman turned when, weary and exhausted with his labors in the courts, the Cabinet or the Senate, he felt the need of rest. He delighted to array himself in a farmer's rough garb, to stride over his own fields, and look after his cattle. He had not forgotten his early tastes, and reveled in the free and unconventional life of this seaside farm. He drank in health from the invigorating seabreezes, and always bore more easily the burden of public cares after a few days at Marshfield.

"I had rather be here than in the Senate," he said on one occasion to his son, while amusing himself with feeding his cattle with ears of corn from an unhusked pile lying upon the barn floor.

Mr. Webster was a keen disciple of Isaac Walton, and spent many an hour with rod and line, when perhaps his thoughts were busy with some intricate political problem, or his mind was occupied with the composition of some speech now famous.

To Mr. Harvey's "Reminiscences" I am indebted for the following anecdote of Mr. Webster, and, indeed, for most that I have said about his country life:

"Soon after Mr. Webster went to Marshfield he was one day out on the marshes shooting birds. It was in the month of August, when the farmers were securing their salt hay. He came, in the course of his rambles, to the Green Harbor River, which he wished to cross. He beckoned to one of the men on the opposite bank to take him over in his boat, which lay moored in sight. The man at once left his work, came over and paddled Mr. Webster across the stream. He declined the payment offered him, but lingered a moment, with Yankee curiosity, to question the stranger.

He surmised who Mr. Webster was, and with some hesitation remarked:

"'This is Daniel Webster, I believe?'

"'That is my name,' replied the sportsman.

"'Well, now,' said the farmer, 'I am told that you can make from three to five dollars a day pleadin' cases up in Boston.'

"Mr. Webster replied that he was sometimes so fortunate as to receive that amount for his services.

"'Well, now,' returned the rustic; 'it seems to me, I declare, if I could get as much in the city pleadin' law cases, I would not be a wadin' over these marshes this hot weather shootin' little birds.'"

Had the simple countryman been told that his companion, who was dressed but little better than himself, was making from thirty to forty thousand dollars annually by these same "law cases," we can hardly imagine the extent of his amazement, or perhaps incredulity.

There is a tradition, and Mr. Webster has confirmed it, that he was one day out on the marsh when his attention was drawn to two young men, evidently from the city, who were standing on one side of a creek which it seemed necessary to cross. They were nicely dressed, and evidently dismayed by the apparent necessity of spoiling their fine clothes in the passage. Seeing a large, rough-looking man, with his pants tucked in his boots, approaching them, their faces brightened as they saw a way out of their dilemma.

"My good man," said one, in an eager but patronizing way, "we are in trouble. Can you help us?"

Mr. Webster looked at the young men and appreciated the situation.

He answered gravely, "What is your difficulty?"

"We want to get across this creek, but you see we might spoil our clothes if we undertook to wade."

Mr. Webster nodded.

"You look like a good, strong fellow, and it won't hurt your clothes. Will you carry us across on your back?"

Mr. Webster's eyes twinkled, but he did not suffer the young men to see it. They were lightly made, and no great burden to one of his herculean frame.

"Yes," he answered; "I will oblige you."

So he took the two over in turn, and deposited them, greatly to their satisfaction, safe and sound on the opposite shore.

"I'm ever so much obliged," said the first. "Here, my man, take this," and he drew half a dollar from his pocket.

The second made the same tender.

"You are quite welcome, young gentlemen," said Mr. Webster; "but I can't think of accepting any recompense."

"Really, though, it's worth it, isn't it, Jones?" said the first young man, addressing his companion.

"Of course it is. Better take the money, sir."

"I must decline," said Mr. Webster, smiling.

"Ever so much obliged. Really, it's very kind of you. By the way, doesn't Daniel Webster live round here somewhere?"

"Yes; you are on his land now," said the rough-looking countryman.

"You don't say so. Is there any chance of seeing him, do you think?"

"A very good chance. *You have only to take a good look at me.*"

"Are—you—Mr.—Webster?" faltered the young men simultaneously.

"Men call me so," answered the statesman, enjoying the confusion of the young men.

They attempted to apologize for the liberty they had taken, and the great mistake they had made, but without much success, and, notwithstanding the good-natured manner in which their excuses were received by Mr. Webster, were glad when they were out of his presence.

I cannot resist the temptation to record another amusing incident in the summer life of Mr. Webster. One day he had gone to Chelsea Beach to shoot wild fowl. While lying among the tall grass, he watched from his concealment the flocks of birds as they flew over the beach and adjacent waters. A flock appeared flying quite low, and he lowered the muzzle of his gun below the horizontal range to bring the birds before his eye. He fired, and instantly there was a loud cry proceeding from the beach below. In alarm, Mr. Webster rushed down the bank, and descried a stranger rubbing his face and shoulder ruefully. The sportsman himself was not looking his best. His raiment was disordered and his face was begrimed with powder.

"My dear sir," he inquired, anxiously, "did I hit you?"

The man answered resentfully, "Yes, you did hit me; *and, from your looks, I should think that I am not the first man you have shot, either.*"

CHAPTER XXXVI.

THE SEVENTH OF MARCH SPEECH.

Were I to undertake a complete account of Mr. Webster's public acts during the last ten years of his life, I should require to write a volume upon this part of his life alone. This does not enter into my plan. I aim only to give my young readers a general idea of the public and private life of the great statesman, and must refer them for particulars to the valuable Life by George Ticknor Curtis, already more than once referred to.

Mr. Webster was strongly opposed to the annexation of Texas, foreseeing that it would justly be resented by the people of the North as tending to increase "the obvious inequality which exists in the representation of the people in Congress by extending slavery and slave representation."

Slavery was the one great flaw in our otherwise glorious system of government. It was a standing reproach among the European nations that a government which claimed to be free held in forcible subjection three million slaves. It sowed dissension between the North and the South, and seemed to be the entering wedge destined ere long to split asunder the great republic. There were men on both sides of Mason and Dixon's line who openly favored separation, but Mr. Webster was not one of these. His ardent devotion to the Union we have already seen in the glowing peroration to his memorable speech against Hayne. He watched with an anxiety which he did not attempt to conceal the growing exasperation of feeling between the the two sections. Though he took the Northern view, he saw that there must be mutual concessions or the Union would be dissolved. He did not wish that event to come in his time, and it was in this frame of mind that he made his last great speech in the Senate—what is known as the seventh of March speech.

It was a strong and temperate statement of the existing condition of affairs, and of the necessity of compromise. In making this speech Mr. Webster was fully aware that he was hazarding his popularity—nay, was sure to lose it—that he would grieve his best friends, and excite a storm of indignation at the North. He was not mistaken. The minds of men were in no mood for temperate counsels. They were in no mood to appreciate the patriotic motives which actuated the great statesman. He was charged with falling from honor and making undue concessions to slavery. Upon this last point I shall express no opinion. I only claim that Mr. Webster's motives were pure, and that though he may have gone too far in his concessions, he was influenced thereto by the depth of his devotion to the Union. There were not wanting those who charged him with making in his speech a bid for the Presidency, forgetting that he could not have injured his chances more effectually than by stirring up against himself his warmest political friends.

That Mr. Webster had an honorable ambition to serve his country in that great office—the greatest in its gift—no one will dispute. He knew his own fitness, and would have rejoiced to crown a life of high service with this elevated trust. But I have said elsewhere that it is only in an ideal republic that the greatest citizens reach the highest posts, and our republic is not an ideal one.

In the light of our present experience we can see that Mr. Webster was wrong in supposing that the repubic could go on indefinitely with slavery as its cornerstone. Any compromise could be only for a time. But he was an old man—sixty-eight years of age—grown cautious and conservative with advancing years, and he could not see through the clouds that gathered before him.

With this brief vindication of his motives, I proceed to give an extract from his last great speech:

"Secession! Peaceable secession! Sir, your eyes and mine are never destined to see that miracle. The dismemberment of this vast country without convulsion! The breaking up of the fountains of the great deep without ruffling the surface! Who is so foolish —I beg everybody's pardon—as to expect any such thing? Sir, he who sees these States now revolving in harmony around a common center, and expects to see them quit their places and fly off without convulsion, may look the next moment to see the heavenly bodies rush from their spheres and jostle against each other in the realms of space, without causing the wreck of the universe! There can be no such thing as a peaceable secession. Peaceable secession is an impossibility. Is the great Constitution under which we live, covering this whole country, is it to be thawed and melted away by secession, as the snows on the mountain melt under the influence of a vernal sun, disappear and run off? No, sir! No, sir! I will not state what might produce the disruption of the Union; but, sir, I see as plainly as I see the sun in heaven what that disruption must produce; I see that it must produce war, and such a war as I will not describe in its two-fold character.

"Peaceable secession! Peaceable secession! The concurrent agreement of all the members of this great government to separate! A voluntary separation with alimony on one side, and on the other! Why, what would be the result? Where is the line to be drawn? What States are to secede? What is to remain America? What am I to be? An American no longer? Am I to become a sectional man, a local man, a separationist, with no country in common with the gentlemen who sit around me here, or who fill the other House of Congress? Heaven forbid! Where is the flag of the republic to remain? Where is the eagle still to tower? or is he to cower and shrink, and fall to the ground? Why, sir, our ancestors, our fathers, and our grandfathers, those of them who are still living among us with prolonged lives, would rebuke and reproach us, and our children and our grandchildren would cry out shame upon us, if we of this generation should dishonor these ensigns of the power of the government and the harmony of the union which is every day felt among us with so much joy and gratitude. What is to become of the army? What is to become of the navy? What is to become of the public lands? How is each of the thirty States to defend itself?

"I know, although the idea has not been stated distinctly, there is to be, or it is supposed possible that there will be, a Southern confederacy. I do not mean, when I allude to this statement, that any one seriously contemplates such a state of things. I do not mean to say that it is true, but I have heard it suggested elsewhere that the idea has been entertained that, after the dissolution of this Union a Southern Confederacy might be formed. I am sorry, sir, that it has ever been thought of, talked of, or dreamed of, in the wildest flights of human imagination. But the idea, so far as it exists, must be of a separation, assigning the slave States to one side, and the free States to the other. Sir, I may express myself too strongly, perhaps, but there are impossibilities in the moral as well as the physical world, and I hold the idea of a separation of these States, those that are free to form one government, and those that are slave-holding to form another, as such an impossibility. We could not separate the States by any such line if we were to draw it. We could not sit down here to-day and draw a line of separation that would satisfy any five men in the country. There are natural causes that would keep and tie us together, and there are social and domestic relations which we could not break if we would, and which we should not if we could."

In describing the consequences of secession it must be admitted that Mr. Webster spoke like a true prophet. All the evils that he predicted—the war such as the world had never seen—came to pass, but out of it the Union emerged stronger than ever, with its chief burden and reproach thrown overboard. Much as the war cost, we feel to-day that we are the better off that it was fought. Let us not blame Mr. Webster that he could not penetrate the future, and strove so hard to avert it. Probably his speech postponed it, but nothing could avert it. Can we doubt that if the great statesman were living to-day he would thank God that He had solved the great problem that had baffled the wisdom of the wisest and brought substantial good from fratricidal strife?

Among those who listened with rapt attention to Mr. Webster was John Calhoun, his great compeer, who had risen with difficulty from the bed where he lay fatally sick, to hear the senator from Massachusetts. "A tall, gaunt figure, wrapped in a long black cloak, with deep, cavernous black eyes, and a thick mass of snow-white hair brushed back from the large brow," he seemed like a visitant from the next world. It was his last appearance in the Senate. Before March was over he had gone to his rest!

CHAPTER XXXVII.

CLOSING SCENES.

Mr. Webster's public life was drawing to a close. After the death of Gen. Taylor he accepted for a second time the post of Secretary of State, but there is nothing in his official work that calls for our special attention. Important questions came up and were satisfactorily disposed of. There was a strong hand at the helm.

June, 1852, brought him a great disappointment. The Whig Convention assembled in Baltimore to nominate a candidate for the Presidency. Mr. Webster was by all means the leader of that party, and was one of the three candidates balloted for. But in the end the successful man was Gen. Winfield Scott. It was a nomination like that of Harrison and Taylor, dictated solely by what was thought to be availability. In this case a mistake was made. Gen. Scott was disastrously defeated by Gen. Franklin Pierce, the nominee of the Democracy.

Gen. Pierce, though parted by politics, was a devoted friend of Mr. Webster, and the reader may be interested to know that on hearing of his nomination, he spoke thus: "Well, all I can say is, and I say it in sincerity, if the people of the United States were to repudiate caucuses, conventions, politicians and tricksters, and rise in the glory of their strength and might, without waiting for any convention to designate a candidate, but bent on placing in the Presidential chair the first citizen and statesman, the first patriot and man, Daniel Webster, it would do for republican government more than any event which has taken place in the history of the world. These are my sentiments, democracy or no democracy."

This is certainly a remarkable tribute from the nominee of one party to an unsuccessful candidate of another, but Gen. Pierce had shown on many occasions his warm friendship and admiration for Mr. Webster.

At Mr. Webster's age it was not likely that he would ever again be a candidate for the Presidency. His last chance had slipped away, and the disappointment was keen. He was already in declining health, induced partly by a severe accident which befell him in May, 1852, when he was thrown headlong to the earth while riding behind a span of horses to Plymouth. Probably the injury was greater than appeared. Towards the end of September, while at Marshfield, alarming symptoms were developed, and his grand physical system was evidently giving way. That month was to be his last. His earthly work was done, and he was never again to resume his work at Washington. The closing scenes are thus described by Mr. Curtis:

"It was past midnight when, awaking from one of the slumbers that he had at intervals, he seemed not to know whether he had not already passed from his earthly existence. He made a strong effort to ascertain what the consciousness that he could still perceive actually was, and then uttered those well-known words, 'I still live!' as if he had satisfied himself of the fact that he was striving to know. They were his last coherent utterance. A good deal later he said something in which the word 'poetry' was distinctly heard. His son immediately repeated to him one of the stanzas of Gray's 'Elegy.' He heard it and smiled After this respiration became more difficult, and at length it went on with perceptible intervals. All was now hushed within the chamber, and to us who stood waiting there were but three sounds in nature: the sighing of the autumn wind in the trees, the slow ticking of the clock in the hall below, and the deep breathing of our dying friend. Moments that seemed hours flowed on. Still the measured beat of time fell painfully distinct upon our ears; still the gentle moaning of the wind mingled with the only sound that arose within the room; for there were no sobs of women, no movements of men. So grand, and yet so calm and simple, had been his approach to the moment when he must know that he was with us no more, that he had lifted us into a composure which, but for his great example, we could not have felt. At twenty-three minutes before three o'clock his breathing ceased; the features settled into a superb repose, and Dr. Jeffries, who still held the pulse, after waiting a few seconds, gently laid down the arm, and amid a breathless silence, pronounced the single word, 'Dead.' The eyes were then closed, the remains were removed from the position in which death came, and all but those who had been appointed to wait and watch slowly and mournfully walked away."

Thus died a man whom all generations will agree in pronouncing great; a man not without faults, for he was human, but one to whom his country may point with pride as a sincere patriot, a devoted son, who, in eloquence at the bar and in the Senate, is worthy of a place beside the greatest orators of any nation, or any epoch. He has invested the name of an American citizen with added glory, for he was a typical American, the genuine product of our republican institutions. No poor boy who reads his life need despair of becoming eminent, for he can hardly have more obstacles to overcome than the farmer's boy, who grew up on the sterile soil of New Hampshire, and fought his way upward with unfailing courage and pluck. Not once in a century is such a man born into the world—a man so amply endowed by his Creator—but he did not rely upon his natural talents, but was a firm believer in hard work. With all his marvelous ability he would not otherwise have left behind him such a name and fame.

CHAPTER XXXVIII.

CENTENNIAL TRIBUTES.

On the 18th of January, 1882, the hundredth birthday of Daniel Webster, the Marshfield Club assembled at the Parker House, in Boston, to take suitable notice of the anniversary. Though thirty years had elapsed since his death there was one at least present, Hon. Robert C. Winthrop, who had been intimately associated with him in public life, having been his successor in the Senate, and a warm personal friend. Most notable among the addresses was that of Gov. Long, of Massachusetts, which I shall venture to insert here, as containing in brief compass a fitting estimate of the great statesman whom the company had assembled to honor.

GOVERNOR LONG'S ADDRESS.

"It is but a poor tribute that even the most eloquent voice, least of all mine, can pay for Massachusetts to the memory of her greatest statesman, her mightiest intellect and her most powerful orator. Among her sons he towers like the lonely and massive shaft on Bunker Hill, upon the base and the crest of which his name is emblazoned clearer than if chiseled deep in its granite cubes. For years he was her synonym. Among the States he sustained her at that proud height which Winthrop and Sam Adams gave her in the colonial and provincial days. With what matchless grandeur he defended her! With what overwhelming power he impressed her convictions upon the national life! God seems to appoint men to special work, and, that done, the very effort of its achievement exhausts them, and they rise not again to the summit of their meridian. So it was with Webster. He knows little even of written constitutions and frames of government who does not know that they exist almost less in the letter than in the interpretation and construction of the letter. In this light it is not too much to say that the Constitution of the United States, as it existed when it carried our country through the greatest peril that ever tested it, was the crystalization of the mind of Webster as well as of its original framers. It came from them and was only accepted by some of our own as a compact of States, sovereign in all but certain enumerated powers delegated to a central government. He made it the crucible of a welded Union—the charter of one great country, the United States of America. He made the States a nation and enfolded them in its single banner. It was the overwhelming logic of his dicussion, the household familiarity of his simple but irresistible statement, that gave us munition to fight the war for the preservation of the Union and the abolition of slavery. It was his eloquence, clear as crystal and precipitating itself in the school-books and literature of a people, which had trained up the generation of twenty years ago to regard this nation as one, to love its flag with a patriotism that knew no faction or section, to be loyal to the whole country, and to find in its Constitution power to suppress any hand or combination raised against it. The great Rebellion of 1861 went down hardly more before the cannon of Grant and Farragut than the thunder of Webster's reply to Hayne. He knew not the extent of his own achievement. His greatest failure was that he rose not to the height and actual stroke of his own resistless argument, and that he lacked the sublime inspiration, the disentanglement and the courage to let the giant he had created go upon his errand, first of force, and then, through that, of surer peace. He had put the work and genius of more than

an ordinary lifetime of service into the arching and
knitting of the Union, and this he could not bear to
put to the final test; his great heart was sincere in
the prayer that his eyes might not behold the earthquake that would shake it to those foundations
which, though he knew it not, he had made so strong
that a succeeding generation saw them stand the
shock as the oak withstands the storm. Men are not
gods, and it needed in him that he should rise to a
moral sublimity and daring as lofty as the intellectual
heights above which he soared with unequaled
strength. So had he been godlike.

"A great man touches the heart of the people as
well as their intelligence. They not only admire,
they also love him. It sometimes seems as if they
sought in him some weakness of our common human
nature, that they may chide him for it, forgive it,
and so endear him to themselves the more. Massachusetts had her friction with the younger Adams
only to lay him away with profounder honor, and to
remember him devotedly as the defender of the right
of petition and 'the old man eloquent.' She forgave
the over-weening conceit of Sumner, she revoked her
unjust censure of him, and now points her youth to
him in his high niche as the unsullied patriot, without fear and without reproach, who stood and spoke
for equal rights, and whose last great service was to
demand and enforce his country's just claims against
the dishonorable trespass of the cruisers of that England he had so much admired. Massachusetts smote,
too, and broke the heart of Webster, her idol, and
then broke her own above his grave, and to-day
writes his name highest upon her roll of statesmen.
It seems disjointed to say that, with such might as
his, the impression that comes from his face upon the
wall, as from his silhouette upon the background of
our history, is that of sadness—the sadness of the
great deep eyes, the sadness of the lonely shore he
loved, and by which he sleeps. The story of Webster
from the beginning is the very pathos of romance. A
minor chord runs through it like the tenderest note
in a song. What eloquence of tears is in that narrative, which reveals in this giant of intellectual

strength the heart, the single loving heart, of a child, and in which he describes the winter sleigh ride up the New Hampshire hills when his father told him that at whatever cost he should have a college education, and he, too full to speak, while a warm glow ran all over him, laid his head upon his father's shoulder and wept!

"The greatness of Webster and his title to enduring gratitude have two illustrations. He taught the people of the United States, in the simplicity of common understanding, the principles of the Constitution and government of the country, and he wrought for them, in a style of matchless strength and beauty, the literature of statesmanship. From his lips flowed the discussion of constitutional law, of economic philosophy, of finance, of international right, of national grandeur and of the whole range of high public themes, so clear and judicial that it was no longer discussion, but judgment. To-day—and so it will be while the republic endures—the student and the legislator turn to the full fountain of his statement for the enunciation of these principles. What other authority is quoted, or holds even the second or third place? Even his few words have imbedded themselves in the common phraseology, and come to the tongue like passages from the Psalms or the poets. I do not know that a sentence or a word of Sumner's repeats itself in our everyday parlance. The exquisite periods of Everett are recalled like the consummate work of some master of music, but no note or refrain sings itself over and over again to our ears. The brilliant eloquence of Choate is like the flash of a bursting rocket, lingering upon the retina indeed after it has faded from the wings of the night, but as elusive of our grasp as spray drops that glisten in the sun. The fiery enthusiasm of Andrews did, indeed, burn some of his heartbeats forever into the sentiment of Massachusetts; but Webster made his language the very household words of a nation. They are the library of a people. They inspired and still inspire patriotism. They taught and still teach loyalty. They are the school-book of the citizen. They are the inwrought and accepted fiber of American politics. If the temple of our republic shall ever fall, they will 'still live' above the ground like those great foundation stones in ancient ruins, which remain in lonely grandeur, unburied in the dust that springs to turf over all else, and making men wonder from what rare quarry and by what mighty force they came. To Webster, as to few other men, is it due that to-day, wherever a son of the United States, at home or abroad, 'beholds the gorgeous ensign of the republic, now known and honored throughout the earth, still full high advanced, its arms and trophies streaming in their original luster, not a stripe erased or polluted, nor a single star obscured,' he can utter a prouder boast than, *Civis Romanus Usum*. For he can say, I am an American citizen."

As a fitting pendant to this eloquent tribute, I quote a portion of the address of Mr. Winthrop, whose name, personally and by inheritance, makes him one of the most eminent sons of Massachusetts:

"And, after all, Mr. President, what are all the fine things which have ever been said of him, or which ever can be said of him, to-night or a hundred years hence, compared with the splendid record which he has left of himself as an advocate in the courts, as a debater in the Senate, as an orator before the people? We do not search out for what was said about Pericles or Demosthenes or Cicero or Burke. It is enough for us to read their orations. There are those, indeed, who may justly desire to be measured by the momentary opinions which others have formed and expressed about them. There are not a few who may well be content to live on the applauses and praises which their efforts have called forth from immediate hearers and admirers. They will enjoy at least a reflected and traditional fame. But Webster will always stand safest and strongest on his own showing. His fame will be independent of praise or dispraise from other men's lips. He can be measured to his full altitude, as a thinker, a writer, a speaker, only by the standard of his own immortal productions. That masterly style, that pure Saxon English, that clear and cogent statement, that close and clinching logic, that power of going down to the depths and up to the neights of any gread argument, letting the immaterial or incidental look out for itself, those vivid descriptions, those magnificent metaphors, those thrilling appeals—not introduced as mere ornaments wrought out in advance, and stored up for an opportunity of display, but sparkling and blazing out in the very heat of an effort, like gems uncovering themselves in the working of a mine—these are some of the characteristics which will secure for Webster a fame altogether his own, and will make his works a model and a study, long after most of those who have praised him, or who have censured him, shall be forgotten.

"What if those six noble volumes of his were obliteratep from the roll of American literature and American eloquence! What if those great speeches, recently issued in a single compendious volume, had no existence! What if those consummate defenses of the Constitution and the Union had never been uttered, and their instruction and inspiration had been lost to us during the fearful ordeal to which that Constitution and that Union have since been subjected? Are we quite sure that we should have had that Constitution as it was, and the Union as it is, to be fought for, if the birth we are commemorating had never occurred—if that bright Northern Star had never gleamed above the hills of New Hampshire? Let it be, if you please, that its light was not always serene and steady. Let it be that mist and clouds sometimes gathered over its disk, and hid its guiding rays from many a wistful eye. Say even, if you will, that to some eyes it seemed once to be shooting madly from its sphere. Make every deduction which his bitterest enemies have ever made for any alleged deviation from the course which he had marked out for it by others, or which it seemed to have marked out for itself, in its path across the sky. Still, still there is radiance and glory enough left, as we contemplate its whole golden track, to make us feel and acknowledge that it had no fellow in our firmament."

THE END.

www.ingramcontent.com/pod-product-compliance
Lightning Source LLC
Chambersburg PA
CBHW010044090426
42735CB00018B/3383